PRAISE FOR *OPENING TO DARKNESS*

"*Opening to Darkness* is beautiful, wise, magical, earthly, and utterly necessary for our time."

RESMAA MENAKEM, MSW, LICSW, SEP
bestselling author of *My Grandmother's Hands*,
The Quaking of America, and *Monsters in Love*

"Zenju shines a contemplative light on the wisdom of sacred darkness, offering a journey of returning to what we have forgotten and must now remember that heals and unites humanity. This book offers life-giving practices to those seeking the revelations of wholeness and belonging."

RUTH KING
author of *Mindful of Race: Transforming
Racism from the Inside Out*

"In these times, what some might call . . . 'dark times,' Zenju Earthlyn Manuel does not offer us a sun, starlight, or even a torch, yet in this book we are lovingly led. As we stumble through the void, running into trees and away from ourselves, we are reminded that, yes, this too can be divine direction. This book beckons us to remember that the sacred nutrients of wisdom, creation, and transformation dwell in blackness, in darkness. Who might we become? What miracles might our world give forth if we learned not only to make peace with the dark but to honor her for all she teaches us about this glorious enigmatic existence of ours? *Opening to Darkness* cradles us with grace in the womb of that ever-pregnant possibility."

SONYA RENEE TAYLOR
activist and author, *New York Times* bestselling
author of *The Body Is Not an Apology*

OPENING TO DARKNESS

ALSO BY
ZENJU EARTHLYN MANUEL

*The Shamanic Bones of Zen: Revealing the Ancestral
Spirit and Mystical Heart of a Sacred Tradition*

The Deepest Peace: Contemplations from a Season of Stillness

The Way of Tenderness: Awakening through Race, Sexuality, and Gender

Seeds for a Boundless Life: Zen Teachings from the Heart
by Zenkei Blanche Hartman (compiled and
edited by Zenju Earthlyn Manuel)

*Tell Me Something about Buddhism: Questions and Answers for
the Curious Beginner* (foreword by Thich Nhat Hanh)

*Black Angel Cards: 36 Oracle Cards and
Messages for Divining Your Life*

Contributing author to:

*The Hidden Lamp: Stories from Twenty-Five Centuries of
Awakened Women*, edited by Florence Caplow and Susan Moon

*Dharma, Color, and Culture: New Voices in Western
Buddhism*, edited by Hilda Gutierrez Baldoquin

OPENING TO DARKNESS

EIGHT GATEWAYS FOR BEING
WITH THE ABSENCE OF LIGHT
IN UNSETTLING TIMES

ZENJU EARTHLYN MANUEL

sounds true
BOULDER, COLORADO

Sounds True
Boulder, CO 80306

Published 2023

Cover design by Huma Ahktar
Book design by Charli Barnes
Illustrations © 2023 Zenju Earthlyn Manuel
Graphic design assistance from Kim Mason

Printed in The United States of America

BK06311

Library of Congress Cataloging-in-Publication Data

Names: Manuel, Zenju Earthlyn, author.
Title: Opening to darkness : eight gateways for being with the absence of
     light in unsettling times / Zenju Earthlyn Manuel.
Description: Boulder, CO : Sounds True, 2023. | Includes bibliographical
     references.
Identifiers: LCCN 2022017208 (print) | LCCN 2022017209 (ebook) | ISBN
     9781683648611 (trade paperback) | ISBN 9781683648628 (ebook)
Subjects: LCSH: Meditation. | Darkness—Psychological aspects.
Classification: LCC BL627 .M344 2023 (print) | LCC BL627
     (ebook) | DDC 158.1/2—dc23/eng20221107
LC record available at https://lccn.loc.gov/2022017208
LC ebook record available at https://lccn.loc.gov/2022017209

FSC
www.fsc.org
MIX
Paper | Supporting
responsible forestry
FSC® C103098

10 9 8 7 6 5 4 3 2 1

What hurts you blesses you. Darkness is your candle.

—Jalāl ad-Dīn Muḥammad Rūmi

CONTENTS

Contents

Contents

PART 1

BEYOND CHALLENGING:
A SHORT PRELUDE

A doctor of Chinese medicine who was a famous bonesetter in China once said to me with a heavy accent, "Here, you [meaning Americans] don't like to feel pain. You don't like to suffer." He said this as he wrung my neck as one would a chicken's, snapping it back and forth in a way I had never experienced. I screamed as if he were breaking my bones.

For a month prior, I hadn't been able to move my head to the left or right. My left arm was nearly immobile. I had just started a new job that probably should have ended the moment my body locked up. I went for acupuncture, then pain pills; used ice and hot water bottles. I went to medical doctors, and they X-rayed the area and gave me more pills and a brace to keep my head still—the kind used for whiplash. I later tried one of the best chiropractors in the city, and she gave me the number of a neurosurgeon, thinking I had a herniated disk and would need surgery. I did not seek out the surgeon and stayed in pain for weeks. Finally, a friend from my job gave me the number of her doctor, the famous bonesetter mentioned above. I called him at 10:00 pm that night. That's how much pain I was in. To my surprise, he answered the phone. He said, "Come in. I wait for you."

I said, "Now?"

"Yes!" he said. "You have pain, come now."

Wow, I thought. *Now that's a healer.* It didn't matter that it was the middle of the night.

My partner at the time drove me across the Bay Bridge to San Francisco, and I met my friend from work at the healer's office. She had come to translate from Mandarin to English. The place was tiny, with photos on the wall of city dignitaries and other famous people who were his clients.

"Hi." The bonesetter smiled like a boy. "I'm Dr. Fu."

I sat down in his small room and showed him my X-ray. He threw it on the floor without looking at it. He took the brace off my neck and threw that on the floor, too, right next to the X-ray. Then he twisted me into a pretzel. I howled, yelped, screamed, and hollered. All of it. No wonder he had me come when no other patients were there. He told me to breathe, and I did my best.

Suddenly, at the peak of the pain, I felt my muscles release in my neck, shoulders, and back. It was in fact a miracle to me. I had suffered so long.

I carried my brace and X-ray out in my hands. It was as if I had never been in pain or unable to move. The night sky filled with stars made me feel like I was on another planet. I was in bliss. When I returned to work, everyone was shocked. Was it a miracle, or was it the ability to withstand a greater amount pain to be free of the pain? I would have never imagined that I needed to go deeper into the pain, deeper into the darkness of it. All I had wanted was out.

We are averse to pain and suffering and understandably so, given our American sensibility. We have access to a large market of remedies, products, spiritual paths, and, yes, gateways to the freedom from suffering. I wonder how many times we have diverted our own freedom when we have discovered there is more pain, more trouble, more darkness ahead and we keep adding on remedies. What is the mindset, along with fear and terror, that causes us to avoid our suffering rather than go deeper into seeing what is there? Yes, I should have quit that job on the spot when the pain started, even though I had been there for only a few weeks. I didn't know at the time, but the pain that was deep inside was because I wanted something different for my life than the job I had accepted. The pain was my impatience, and it was at the same time physical pain in real time. I didn't wait to allow that "something different" to be revealed in the darkness.

Since all paths—religious, spiritual, or without name—intersect in the place of darkness, darkness is the place where the mind is forced to detach itself from whatever it has grabbed onto in life. And in that nothingness, in that dark place, we awaken.

What of darkness terrorizes us so that we run from it, rather than go deeper into it? How can we bear dark times, or, more explicitly, horrifying times, with the skill of an awakened one? Misery, struggle, and sorrow are not the sole intentions of this life. Yet we can respect our interrelationship with everything in the world, including the suffering in, around, and between us. Is there a way to live in unsettling times that we have forgotten?

THE ART OF DARKNESS

While darkness and lightness have been rooted in our physical, emotional, social, and spiritual lives, it is the spiritual impact of darkness on our lives and how we suffer—with and in it—that this book addresses. How can we meet darkness as itself, alone, not as an opposition to the light we long for? What is darkness without an attention to light or our longing for light? When I ask questions like these, suddenly there are no words. Darkness without talking about light makes darkness inconceivable to many. It is much like the darkness of death. We do not know death any more than the darkness we came from. But we speak of a darkness that is not there—it doesn't really exist except in our perception. Still, there is this experience of what we call darkness that is so palpable we run from it, hide in it, and often seek ways to annihilate it. We speak of light, but we are not sure of light in the same way that we are not sure of darkness. Is the absence of light the nature of life?

Kerry James Marshall, an artist featured in the 2021 documentary *Black Art: In the Absence of Light*, is known for the black-velvety-looking skin of the people he paints in his work. He uses different pigments to create a wordless form of the absence of light. In Marshall's famous painting *A Portrait of the Artist as a Shadow of His Former Self*, the charcoal-black-faced man in the painting is nearly invisible except for the white of his eyes and teeth. But the white of his eyes exists only because of the black skin. The viewer is forced to look into the white to see the black, to even see the person. Marshall depicts his reality of being seen and not seen as a dark-skinned man.

We all create an image in our minds in which we see darkness and feel it. We believe darkness exists as we imagine it. We see a dark room, a night sky, a black sweater and imagine something in regard to darkness. At the same time, we can be unsure of darkness. How could darkness be both certain and not, seen and unseen? What is this darkness without light that affects our relationship to the earth and to each other? What is this absence of light that can cause suffering inside a myriad of life experiences? Do we see the white of the eyes and teeth without the darkness that surrounds it?

In this book, I make an effort to connect these rhetorical or abstract questions on darkness with Eight Gateways of being with darkness and ways of being with dark experiences in our lives. Our soul needs dark experiences to ascend, to evolve into a consciousness of vastness in every moment. I have gathered the teachings over the years on many paths of walking a spiritual life, and all of my spiritual transmissions are integrated here in this book. You may recognize the root of Zen Buddhism and the influence of African and Native American indigenous traditions, lucid prophetic dreaming, ceremonial drumming, and more.

YOU ARE THE MANDALA

The mandala you're going to explore in this book was a long time coming. In a lucid dream many years ago, I was seated, with several other people, on a colorful marble floor with paintings of deities in red, blue, yellow, and green. I was unaware of the reason I had been called to the gathering. None of us present knew one another. I looked about. There were pillars but no walls nor ceiling in the room we were seated in. It was an open temple in which the sun and blue sky beamed over our heads. We waited quietly until a being came to greet us. I say "being" because, while appearing as a person, it did not feel like one. The being gave one instruction to all of us: "Create a mandala of your teachings." I sat still and did nothing throughout the dream. This was long before the creation of my oracle cards, which also came in a lucid dream; long before I was ordained as a Zen priest. I did not know how to move forward.

While being artistic, mandalas of all traditions are usually symbolic expressions of our inner worlds. It is only in writing this book, decades later, that I have finally come to the mandala of darkness that has been with me for my entire life. Unknowingly, I had been speaking of it while sharing with others the experience of navigating dark times. I had been walking it with each footstep circling the vast meadow of life.

The mandala in this book appears on the page, but it is created as you travel through the Eight Gateways. You'll find guided stillness exercises to help you experience a mandala of darkness within you. *You* will be the mandala as you walk through these gateways. Hopefully, you will access the authentic nature of darkness within you despite the distortions imposed on darkness that are learned and experienced by everyone. Figure 1 is an outer representation of the mandala as you move through the gateways. For now, just feel what comes up when you look at it. Take some time to study it before reading the description below.

Figure 1. The mandala with the Eight Gateways

The eight dragons on the outside circle of the mandala represent the fire of darkness and protection. They also represent the Buddha's Eightfold Path for the cessation of suffering, which will be discussed later. The outlined background of the lotus flower symbolizes our lives in the midst of mud, dark periods, or unsettling times.

Also in the mandala there are depictions of dark mothers or deities within particular gateways (see table 1).

OUTER RING			
GATEWAY	**DIRECTION**	**THEME**	**DARK MOTHER**
First	East	The Nature of Darkness	Mahakali/ Daikokutennyo (Indian Hinduism/ Japanese Buddhism)
Second	South	Sensing in the Wilderness of Darkness	Mama Black Panther (Nature)
Third	West	Childhood Fear of Darkness	Mama Dantor (Haitian)
Fourth	North	Dwelling in Darkness	Mami Wata (Benin, formerly Dahomey)
INNER RING			
GATEWAY	**DIRECTION**	**THEME**	**DARK MOTHER**
Fifth	North	Being Messengers of Darkness	Mother Ala (Nigerian/Igbo Odinani)
Sixth	West	Darkness as Light	Papa Damballah (Haitian/West African)
Seventh	South	Understanding "Evil" and Darkness	Mama Erzulie Je Rouj (Haitian)
Eighth	East	Celebrating the Darkness of Death and Birth	Mama Brijit (Haitian)

Table 1. The outer and inner rings of dark mothers

As you read the descriptions in table 1, please keep in mind that I *divined* the directions. They are not the directions in which any particular tradition might place a deity. I use the term *dark mothers* to encompass deities, spirits, gods, goddesses, and African orishas. Know that some African religions have one deity, and that is God. Also, imagine the center circle of elements rotating in the middle, so that the elements affect all deities and at the same time.

I am deliberately *not* using the direct teachings of other traditions in which I have not been authorized. However, in the descriptions of the deities, I do borrow from others to mine the characteristics of the deities as they relate to darkness. Rarely are "darkness" and "deities" spoken in the same breath. What do they say that can help us with darkness? Know that I am completely following the voices of ancestors and there is an effort here to hold all integrity of all paths. Perhaps the ancestors are seeking to change how we practice. I am here for that effort. I already see the needed integration of the fragmented spiritual and religious paths that many of us walk. At the same time, I honor the need to transmit these paths as many have done for centuries. Please try to drop all knowing for now and return later. If you go toward teachings only to see what you already know, then you might miss what could bring new insights to you. See how confusion can lead to discovery.

In the mandala, you'll also see the motifs of four elements in the center circle: fire (east), earth (south), wind (west), and water (north). I have situated them in the middle to illustrate their impact on all of the gateways. Again, imagine the element circle rotating in the center. Although fire appears on the eastern side of the circle, fire isn't exclusive to the east gateway. The element of fire impacts all directions and affects all eight gateways. This is the same for all the other elements symbolized in the center.

THE DARK ROAD WITHIN

This journey is not a call to those who want to stay in what they think is light in order to avoid being negative or being consumed by the dark where monsters and monstrous things live. It is not for those who think they can give light through their words, songs, or cheery dispositions. It is not for those who want to remain wedded to the fear and/or are not willing to reconsider that which they were taught in relationship to darkness. This call is not for those who are interested in sustaining some imagined protection from darkness. It is for the brave ones, the ones who remember living in dark times as a place of power and clear seeing.

Many people are unfamiliar with the authentic nature of darkness. When we conjure darkness, it can be from the two extremes: from horror, danger, and negativity or from abundance, peace, stillness, and beauty. I decided to address in this book the terrorizing aspects of darkness because it is more palpable and grounded in lived experience than the more positive abstract attributes mentioned above. I'm going to venture out on a limb and say that most people have been taught about and speak of darkness as bad, as shadow, as something to be avoided. They unconsciously transfer these attributes to anything black as well. Usually, we don't include the word "blackness" when we say "darkness." I will include it in this text for the sole purpose of illuminating their oneness. I will talk more about this later. For now, please stop, breathe, and consider doing the following exercise.

Take some time now to write down the attributes you give to darkness and blackness. Note if any of those characteristics or descriptions of darkness and blackness fall in the realm of distortion handed down for centuries. Be honest. Are the attributes you give to darkness the true darkness? Are you discovering that you have no words, that honestly you don't know darkness?

It's the twenty-first century, and it feels like we are returning to the beginning, to the dark origin from which humans emerged. The trouble in the world is asking us to assess and recreate how we live. Along the way, we lost track of the stars and now find ourselves in fear of one another, of living and dying, and of the consequences of the human being's impact on the planet we live on. The greatest question is "What will happen to us next?" What if there is no next? We are here, still in the forever darkness and blackness. What if we don't emerge from it as we thought or were taught we would? It is my experience that we come from the inexplainable darkness of birth into a life that is also dark and unknown.

Some might say this book is an attachment to darkness as an idea—a concept. But attachment can also be confused with connection. It's a fine line. So I would like to say that this offering comes from *a deep connection* to the primordial darkness that we are birthed from. It is a connection to an ancient lineage of living with darkness and blackness. I hope to disrupt how we suffer pervasive darkness and blackness in our lives and to illustrate that the way out of such darkness is the way in. The dark road within has been blocked with incomplete or the absence of sacred transmissions for being with darkness. If there is any attachment, it is for all of us to see our way through life without longing for light.

SEVERED FROM ESSENTIAL
DARKNESS AND BLACKNESS

Exploring darkness is not for everyone. But it is spiritual work that is needed as we come to understand how darkness and blackness have been rendered negative, fearful, and to be avoided. Some have reframed the meaning of darkness and blackness, but this doesn't mean that the experience of such has changed. The existence of darkness in our lives and in the world has been used to distort and undermine darkness as well as to promote and justify the purity of lightness. Many recognize the need to heal from such justification by reframing darkness into something positive, but such acts have so far not eliminated centuries of a collective consciousness in which darkness is most often (not always) rendered as the hell realms of life. And most, if not all, of us are not interested in a life in hell—wherever hell is. Perhaps the fear created around hell must also be examined in an effort to shift hundreds of years of deception and create an environment on this planet of desired wellness. What if hell is not a horrible place some speak of but rather the sacred environment of initiation in the interest of wellness?

This exploration is not only a discourse on darkness in an existential sense but also an application of an embodied experience for everyone—internally and externally. Within each of us, darkness is embodied, whether we acknowledge its existence or not. Simply being born from darkness has anchored an experience of it within us. I make this statement so that those who are not embodied in dark skin understand that when I address darkness and blackness it is in relationship to every human being, especially since there is a relationship of darkness and blackness to lightness and whiteness.

The inclusion of blackness with darkness in my exploration was necessary, as I live in a dark and black body. When I say "darkness," I mean "blackness," too, and when I say "blackness," I mean "darkness" as well. These states of being are interchangeable for me and maybe for others. It was impossible to untangle the essence of darkness and an actual life experience of blackness in my exploration. In my writing of this book, the overlay of blackness on darkness or of whiteness on lightness was palpable. We are all aware that we have used these terms and the attributes to describe one another as people throughout time and even more so in the last decade. We have even created light supremacy among everyone, despite skin color. It is this supremacy that makes it important to explore beneath the words and the experiences attached to the words in order to transform and heal the fear and anxiety around darkness and blackness and its being rendered inferior to lightness and whiteness. And to explore our dark experiences so that when faced with them we are not looking for light but rather being with the darkness provided as ground for transformation and renewal.

The existence of darkness and blackness in all of our lives and in the world has been used to distort and undermine darkness and blackness as well as to promote and justify the purity of lightness and whiteness. When we don't examine the distorted history and spirituality of darkness, we lose the unencumbered, unpoliticized, and unadulterated purpose and profound existence of darkness in its organic, everlasting, profound absence of light. The impact of this loss is then projected onto dark experiences, dark people, dark things, and so on. To hold darkness and blackness without the elevation of light and whiteness, even for a moment, is to comprehend a fuller and more distinct aspect of darkness and blackness that we can learn from instead of run from.

Our disconnection from essential darkness and blackness has created pervasive terror and anxiety when we are up against *what* and *who* is considered dark or black. But more importantly, the severance has stunted the growth of humanity and has moved us further away from ascension—from what we are already awake to. We are born with a fear of darkness as a valuable instinct. It was originally a capacity to be used in surviving the forest, open land, and sea. When this primal fear is intensified by things in our contemporary lives, the terror of darkness—a terror wired within us since birth—can cause us to eliminate anything and everything dark in our lives. In essence, the sight of darkness and blackness or the feel of darkness can trigger an ancient primal response to eliminate, to kill in various ways, or to annihilate darkness and blackness without seeing that there is no need to do so. The appearance of darkness and blackness doesn't always signal danger. It may be exactly the dark experience needed or the dark person (in mood or body) needed at the time to help us navigate life. When we seek to eliminate darkness, we remove the place, the womb, in which we awaken. To reclaim the purity of darkness and blackness is to recall its role in shaking us loose of who we think we are or what we think is happening in life.

Fortunately, many spiritual paths use darkness as a portal: in vision quests, cave dwelling during initiations, symbolic burials, sweat lodges, dark meditation halls, or initiations in the dark woods. These portals help us reconcile our abandonment of darkness and blackness, as well as feelings of being overwhelmed by them. In the same vein, I provide various gateways in this book to assist you in opening to the absence of light as a portal for transformation and healing.

As a young adult, I often felt that I had been buried alive in an ancient past life. It was a visceral feeling. I sensed the dirt being piled over my body and me screaming but unheard. I would shake this awful vision from my head every time it showed itself. Later, I wondered why I might have been buried alive. Had I been in a trance and everyone thought I was dead and they had buried me by mistake? Had I done something wrong in a past lifetime and I was remembering the punishment that I carried? Finally, one afternoon the vision took over, and I found myself wailing alone in my home. In the middle of the crying, I went deep into the darkness of my burial vision, trembling and feeling cold. Then, suddenly, I saw my mother's hands, and she, too, was shaking. It was then I realized that instead of being buried alive, I was seeing myself in my mother's womb, waiting to be born.

THE COLLECTIVE EXPERIENCE
OF WHAT'S DARK

Perhaps something is always in the dark waiting to be born repeatedly in the interest of change and transformation, both personal and collective. The more darkness, the more change. I am writing at a time in which there are increasing acts of anti-black and anti-Asian violence, killings of Native American indigenous women, and assaults against immigrants of color. In addition, COVID-19 and its many variants continue to rock our world.

We are living in what many have called a Great Darkness. As humans, we have always been vulnerable to massive wipeout, be it through contaminated food, medicine, climate change, profiled policing, militarism, or war.

There is a silent scream in my head when I hear about genocide, violence of all types, dehumanization against anyone, folks losing their homes to wildfires and floods, the pushing of the poor into refugee status in their homes—urban regions included. This scream has motivated my exploration and creation of a path to reconcile our fear and abandonment of darkness and blackness. Recently, my tears do not come as often in this dark world. Instead, my eyes are fixed wide open, searching for what I may not be able or ready to see. My dry lips are sealed together. There is no spit to fling in rage. And there is no sign or proof that we will be any better or more divine human beings for the depth of our suffering. No matter how many of us—including those who teach, console, and guide—have dedicated our lives to walking ourselves and others to a place of solace and awakening, we are mostly companions in this world of darkness. What is this experience of darkness, and how are we to live through it day after day? There is no one answer. We cannot know until we live through it. But how does one live through deep terror without being able to scream? Or, if we can scream, what if no one hears us? What if they hear but can't help us?

I don't have any answers, but I do have responses. When dark experiences arrive in our lives, we may feel we are facing death when in fact something is trying to be born in us and into the world. Even when we are dying, something is being born in our death—something unknown that will bring a change no human being can create. Newness is constantly coming forth each day of our lives. Often, we fear not knowing what is about to enter. Should we greet it or turn it away? We become anxious and beg for light so that we can see what is about to be born before it comes, or we want to know what is going to happen before it happens. We want to hold on to something in this edgeless, watery darkness.

If you picked up this book, there is something in your bones that understands the power of darkness. You are courageous and strong at heart. Not because darkness is intense, but because you have a willingness to challenge what you think you know about darkness and blackness and face any fear. Or, if you are not afraid, you are willing to consider your love of darkness and blackness. But think about how your love for it serves you and perhaps only you at the expense of a collective love and celebration in our world.

What would it be like if we learned to love the forever darkness, without wanting it to serve us in some way, give us something, or without waiting for what's dark to lighten up? What would it mean if we dwelled in darkness, available to the transformation, much like we did in our mother's womb? What if we welcomed darkness as an ambiguous state of being alive?

The darkness we experience throughout life, although felt as shadowy or unbearable, is more than that. Darkness provides a sacred environment by which we can receive our very life that is forever in the dark from the moment we are born. Dare I say, life is a dark experience—a magical experience. You don't know what is going to happen next, and you didn't know the things in the past were going to happen to you. Most likely the dark caused distress or even despair, especially if the darkness appeared life-threatening. Few people find joy in dark experiences, and many do not even enjoy the darkness of night.

Throughout my spiritual walk, I have come to settle with the discomfort of darkness and to enjoy the curiosity of its presence in my life. I cannot see what can only be discovered in time. When someone says, "That was dark," I get excited for what is about to be born into the world. At the same time, I grow still, stay curious, and remain on the edge of it all with butterflies in my belly. What is it that will come and destroy the "me" I think I know? Andrew Harvey, a modern-day mystic, said in a podcast on darkness, "When the whole of your being, when your time comes for you to be killed by the divine, you will surrender to mystery, and the real divine consciousness can come through you."[1] In being "killed by the divine," there is no more seeing oneself as a thing, an object. In such a state you are to open to darkness, the darkness of the divine consciousness. I would go as far as to say it is to open to a God that is not an object, a person, or a thing. It is to be enlightened without enlightenment being something you have accomplished.

All life comes from darkness. Darkness is unknown, as a divine consciousness is unknown or indescribable. Yet we use the words *dark* and *black* for experiences such as prolonged mistreatment based on skin color, pandemics, war, poverty, death, illness, and so on. Many have written on the abundance and beauty of darkness and the protectors in the dark. But still darkness is unknown. This makes the exploration of it difficult and writing about it even more difficult. Nonetheless, I have taken up the challenge to explore how opening to darkness can ease disdain toward others or to collective devastation or tragedy. Even though darkness has been praised and held as worthy and beneficial by many in various traditions, such a view doesn't seem to transfer to a love for darkness and blackness, or a wonderment in dark experiences. It doesn't seem to lessen the fear of it in our lives.

What about a kind of darkness that is a mirror of life itself, both physically and metaphysically? What about the dark that has gone unloved in the shadow of light? What about darkness as an open field of illumination?

AN UNKNOWN DARKNESS

If there is a darkness that exists and is unknown, then there is a darkness that cannot be eliminated with physical or metaphysical light. When I say "light," I speak of a nonphysical light that resides in darkness and cannot be defined, seen with the eyes, or controlled.

The dark experience of life neither comes nor goes. It is not like how day and night appear and depart. Even if we say that dark and light exist and are experienced daily, darkness and light are one in that they hold what is to be born. In this sense what is revealed in so-called light may be darker than you expect.

How do you honor darkness? Who or what would help you befriend the dark long enough for you to discover the unimaginable? Maybe you are someone who grows anxious with dark experiences, dark people, dark places, dark thoughts, and nothing has helped to heal the trauma and anxiety. Is it possible to be open enough to allow darkness to teach you without longing for light?

We want to corral and eliminate pandemics. We want peace to prevail over war. We want to suck the breath from oppression. We want our personal suffering to lift. We want to get out of darkness so much we may leave it prematurely. Some of us superficially bring ourselves into the light or at least our idea of it. We say, "I have come through it" or "I'm no longer held down." Even if you open to darkness, the light you seek from it cannot come from your mind. It must come from continuously being in the dark, as we have done all our lives without escape. It is like having to live in black skin forever. There is nothing that can take darkness away, fix our trauma, or dispense with our suffering. Our primal nature cries out to be lifted out of darkness, as a mother might lift her frightened baby. If there were something—some religion, some healing modality—that could remove all suffering, it would be sold in a purple pill at the price of a house. So what is this insurmountable chaos and suffering we experience today? What do we do with darkness, with dark times? Learn how to see through them, use them to understand life. Learn how to live fully despite darkness.

We can allow darkness to wake us up and guide us without methods and formulas, and we can do so without the idea that darkness or dark experiences are the worst things that could happen. What are the false ideas that you hide in the dark about yourself? In attending to suffering, are you relying on the unstable "I" that vacillates according to circumstances that also are not stable? Collectively, I sense we are being asked to stand up when the chaos is so thick that we have no idea what to do with it. We are being asked to see, collectively, in the dark and see what it is trying to tell us. It is time to grow out of primal screaming as habit and use it only when necessary. Perhaps in the moment you and I—or at least those parts of us that think we know everything—are being killed by the divine.

When it is suggested to open, go into, and dwell in darkness and blackness, an ancestral fear may surface. We fear what we can't see. We fear the unknown. This ancient fear needs quieting if only for the sake of creating an authentic ascended humanity and to cease the elimination of darkness and blackness. So you might feel disconcerted as you shift your relationship with darkness here, because what has been asserted as true to you about darkness in the past was often distorted. If we knew darkness, we would not fear it. The fear addressed here is not specifically that of severe phobia, clinical depression, anxiety, or other psychological condition or mental illness that can be extreme. Those are to be attended to by professional mental health caretakers. Terror may even be at play for many of us and may also require support of some kind. In this book, the exploration of darkness, which by now you know includes dark experiences, is a historical, cultural, philosophical, and spiritual exploration of the fear of darkness and the fear of a distorted sense of darkness embedded in us as children. Personally, my hope is that this work will also save the lives of people deemed black, dark, or other than white from those triggered by a false sense of darkness and blackness all over the world.

HONORING DARKNESS

What if for a moment we consider that the dark is the light, a different kind of light? It is not the bright light that we think we know and love, but a dark light that is dispersed through a porous, dark fabric. We can't look through this black fabric with our physical eyes. We can only sense it from within. Michael Meade, storyteller and mythologist, said on an episode of his *Living Myth* podcast titled "The Darkness Around Us": "In facing the darkness together we rekindle the divine spark of life in each of our souls."[2] Meade teaches the light inside darkness *is* the human soul. He affirms that we can't create the light out of darkness, as it is already within us.

Opening to darkness is an inner journey with opening to life—an entrance into the vastness of life—opening without grasping for what can't be grasped. Darkness is the birthplace from which all things and all people emerge into being and to which all will reenter at some point in the future. We can't touch that. What is arising from darkness sometimes feels like the worst of the worst. Can we discern if the monsters on our backs are growling because we have yet to give them attention? Who or what are we ignoring in the rise of hatred? What is it that we are still unaware of?

What happened to the original teachings of darkness, which came from being in darkness eons ago? Are we still operating from the manipulated views of darkness created by those who needed an evil darkness to serve them or those who needed everything dark to be eliminated? In the twenty-first century we are being challenged with ever-increasing situations that could cause us to lose heart, lose hope. But it is time to recall and relearn the ancient rituals, ceremonies, and medicines used to ease the terror that emerges in unsettling times.

Darkness will prevail all of our days. What if we are taught to face darkness rather than fight it, suppress it, or dissolve it with some kind of light?

If we learn how to dwell in darkness—and for some of us that includes being in our dark skins—we are less anxious about the lack of light, lack of goodness, lack of anything, period. Even when harmful forces are at work in our minds in dark times, our bodies will lead us, if we let them, to the birthing. Whether we like or dislike what arrives in darkness is superficial. What and who inevitably appear in the world do so for the sake of healing, transformation, and awareness.

The existence of darkness has lost its value in many minds. Although darkness comes to us every day, it has lost its sacred capacity to guide our lives. Early in the history of humanity, when darkness was made largely a place of sorrow, dread, and something to fear, it lost its worth. The origin of an unwelcomed and diminished purpose of darkness happened eons ago within cultures everywhere. The introduction of a specific kind of light, as we see it in the Western world, emerged from early stories telling us that we were in complete darkness until light was introduced. The sun and the moon were separated in concept, which divided darkness from light. This caused great suffering and longing for light. In separating the dark from the light, darkness lost its place in the creation of goodness in humanity and became subject to fear. Some literature, both religious and cultural, has continued to perpetuate this perception of darkness as separate from light and as the worst thing possible to encounter. It has helped create the notion of salvation, to be saved from darkness, on our spiritual and religious paths.

At times, rulers of governments conspired together to rid their societies of what was deemed evil and aligned themselves with the view of darkness as something to watch out for and control. For example, the oppression of anything or anyone black. When the greater darkness was distorted, it robbed blackness of its beauty, expansiveness, and mystery. What we are left with are emotional responses such as disdain or a self-fulfilling love for blackness. We are left with the trauma of experiencing darkness without ceremony and ritual and with little assistance other than the promise of light.

From the beginning of humanity, darkness has been tangled with our emotions—how we feel about the dark. These emotions are transferred into our experience of darkness, moving us further and further away from the dark earth. We are led away from developing a relationship with darkness, and so we fear it and make no inquiries about it. All some of us know is, darkness doesn't feel good.

I asked a neighbor if they could love darkness. They immediately backed away, dropped their head, and said, "No, I can't do that." I responded, "And there it is. How are we going to live in a world that is abundantly dark when we have an aversion to everyone and everything dark in our lives?" They were silent as I stood looking into space. I saw their reaction as primal, influenced by what they had been taught and not taught. I witnessed them, in the moment, grappling with the seeds of a defiled darkness they lived with.

CREATION WITHIN DARKNESS

You might experience some confusion or question efforts here to bring darkness higher into our consciousness. I admit it was difficult to write about something so intangible. I also confess that I encountered an entanglement within me because of the ways darkness has been used and misused. The use of darkness to stand for almost anything unwanted or anything mysterious causes confusion.

Given that I live in a dark-skinned body that is surrounded by dark experiences, including mistreatment based on skin color, I had been hearing the call for decades, through great pain, to open even wider the gateway of darkness for myself and others. Darkness at first had been a place of despair, but through many ceremonies and rituals it became a place of renewal, birthing, and creativity. Darkness fed my rage *and* created poetry. The civil rights movement invited me to love my black skin, to see the dark experiences as a journey into freedom—freedom of the soul. My opening to darkness was a spiritual awakening to the truth of a dynamic darkness, one that was not stripped of soul and essential nature. From this awareness, darkness had so much more to say to me, and I found so much more to uncover about how to live when there is an absence of light.

The words began bursting through me in the spring of 2020 with a pandemic and then the murder of several black people at the hands of those who hate or carry self-hatred. The killings would bring many to enact legislation, defund and reform the police, increase awareness through programs of social justice movements intertwined with spiritual practice, and more. The pandemic would bring vaccines. But what would protect us from increasing death by violence and disease? All of us, regardless of race, gender, sex, heritage, class, et cetera, were being alerted in 2020. While we had external solutions, our attention was being turned toward the fact that human beings would die in as many ways as possible and be destroyed—that darkness would intensify—until we learned how to engage it, see and know it as the transformative soil of our lives. We are being called to cease fighting the dark and wishing for some kind of light that is self-created and perceived as more enjoyable. We are being forced to be more conscious of the darkness humanity was born out of and still lives in.

MEDICINE OF THE DARK MOTHERS

In the San (aka Bushmen) tradition of Namibia, there's a story of a !Kung shaman named Old K"xau.[3] Before Old K"xau was a shaman, Kauha (the God presence) approached him, and, noting that the people were singing, Kauha asked Old K"xau why he wasn't dancing. Before Old K"xau answered, Kauha took him to the other world of spirits and ancestors, where some were engaged in a dance. The shaman began dancing, too. But Kauha stopped him and said, "Don't just come and dance." Kauha told Old K"xau to lie down and watch how he danced. After that, Old K"xau was taken to his protector, who put n/um (healing medicine) into him.

In the San tradition, n/um can emerge only through intense dancing and with the heat of fire. Its heat travels up the spinal cord and enters the head. Once it enters there, the healer can use this n/um to extract illness from others.

Our n/um medicine begins with the dance. Our dancing partner is suffering. We dance in the dark throughout our lives.

The medicine to heal comes through us but isn't decided upon by us. It will come from the dark, not from our knowing of how to do this or that. It took me a while, if not most of my life, to discover that guardianship of all dark experiences, things, and people is a sacred act. We are to uplift darkness—not to uplift over anything, but to simply uplift. We are to stand at the gateway of darkness and witness the birthing from it as it reveals what we need. In doing such, I discovered that the craziness of oppression had legs and that it crawled and moved along, if only to lead us to awareness and enlightenment. Oppression was not a stagnant darkness but an evolutionary one that revealed many times, within and without, that we had not yet experienced grace.

One night, while drumming alone in the dark in front of my fireplace, I started singing to my blood ancestors, to ancestor Earth, and to other planets as ancestors. I had just moved to New Mexico, and it was my first birthday outside of my native state of California, the only place I had ever lived. I was born in the late night on October 31 in the deep, murky water of a scorpion constellation, in water that was in space, surrounded by sky and stars. So I generally expect that something is going to be born to me around that day every year. The drum rhythms strengthened the further away I got from remembering that it was my birthday. The vibration of the drum caused the flames to dance. I drummed harder and sang louder. I continued drumming until exhausted. I walked over to my ancestors' altar with only the photos of my mother and father and gave thanks for my life.

The next day, I was aware that several deities and animal spirits had been showing up in my life in various ways out of the blue (which means out of the darkness) over many years. They seem to come during dark periods of my life. The Black Angel oracle deck I created was drawn from the first group of dark spirits that came to me. They came in a lucid dream. There was a dark side to them that many were not attracted to, although many were. There was an attention to darkness in the medicine of the cards. I knew this darkness as a black woman and felt the medicine of the oracle to be for black women in particular. But the Black Angel image was broader than the blackness of the skin or black women. I knew this. There was a message of darkness that I couldn't quite write about until now. The message of darkness was for everyone but might be understood by those who lived in dark-skinned bodies or those who felt the sting of hatred.

In writing this book, I began to see the Black Angels in my deck as *dark mothers*, an archetype used in women's spirituality, pagan traditions, and some Buddhist traditions. I reflected back on the archetypes in my oracle and felt that I forced the light upon them, especially at the instruction of friends and family. The black part of the angels was troubling to some, while the angel part was imagined as some kind of winged being of heaven. At this writing, I reclaim the darkness they were bringing attention to at the time. I reclaim the reflection of wounding in the dark in the original messages that came through on a night decades ago. I can now see that the wounding addressed in the oracle was deemed the sleeping path and negative to some extent. But the wounding now feels to be from not understanding darkness and not knowing how to use it in our ascension.

The symbol of dark mothers has existed since long before any organized religion or form of spirituality. In essence, the dark mother as archetype is primordial, and it is in this place in which I experience dark mothers and not so much through religion or any specific spirituality. The primordial dark mothers are often presented in powerful female entities, spirits, deities, or goddesses who will shake up our world when we are out of alignment with the earth, when we are not connected to what is well. These dark mothers are seen in many cultures and religious traditions. Their main quality is fierceness, and they are often associated with harshness and love at the same time. The archetypal dark mothers found in many religious traditions have not had their day of importance in our broader spiritual or religious landscape.

Some dark mothers have been celebrated in feminist, religious, and pagan communities. The most well-known dark mother with the capacity for both destruction and peace is Mahakali (Kali), present in various forms in the Hindu and Buddhist traditions. A dharma sister and Zen priest introduced Daikokutennyo to me as the Japanese version of Mahakali. In studying Daikokutennyo (*dai* meaning "great" and *koku* meaning "blackness"), I began to understand a greater blackness that is not an identity but an all-embracing dark spirit—a Daikoku (god) or Daikokutennyo (goddess). Therefore, I included Mahakali in this work as a dark mother. It was the beginning of seeing the existence of dark mothers beyond the Black Madonna, Mary Magdalene, or Demeter.

It is important that I share briefly my personal spiritual and religious journey here so that it is clear how I am using the medicine of dark mothers. I am aware of the Buddhist dark mothers, such as the blue-black Tara (Jetsun Dölma) or Hariti, the loving wrathful protector. These dark mothers have been written about to a great extent by seasoned practitioners and teachers of Vajrayana Buddhist traditions. Since my relationship with these dark mothers is still in development and I am primarily a Soto Zen practitioner, I asked myself which dark mothers I resonate with, which ones match the fierceness I feel in my own body. As you will find in this book, I gravitate toward the dark mothers of Africa. But it is important to say that, in many African religions, practitioners do *not* refer to the spirits I name in this book as dark mothers. I'm overlaying the dark mother archetype from women's spirituality and Buddhism upon the dark mothers of Africa and other continents. As I mentioned previously, I also use the word *deities* at times, whereas many African religious practitioners would consider that there is only one deity, and that is God, but not a Christian God. The dark mothers I present here are from India, Japan, Haiti, Dahomey, and Nigeria. I am not an authorized teacher of the African traditions I borrow from here, nor is "my head made" (the term for ordination) in those practices at this writing. Although I have been called and invited to go forth into priesthood in two African traditions, that process has not been achieved to date. My foundation in this work is having participated in ritual and ceremony for many years. I am by birth and heritage a descendant of those who preserve and serve African spirituality. It was my deep curiosity, personal seeing, and dreaming that provide a field of integration for the teachings here. It made sense for Haitian spirits to come forth and stand at the gateway with me, guiding this offering, as my blood lineage goes back to Haiti by way of Louisiana. It made sense for Nigerian and Dahomean mothers to enter my vision, as I have experienced ceremony from both countries.

Specifically, I have a long mystical experience with Christianity. My Zen priesthood and teacherhood is wide and deep, meaning it has been many years of walking the path and it has been a path with many temples. Although as of this writing I am rooted in Zen, I often see and experience these paths as integral. In this there is no loss of purity in traditions for me but rather an enhancement of one with the other. As one who guards the forms of various practices, I understand the need to safeguard longstanding ancient paths as laid down by the ancestors. And it is important that I share with respect and stay as close to the root of the tradition as possible.

I welcome the many deities who have presented themselves to me through visions, dreams, and divination—to be known and revered in this work on darkness. The deities as dark mothers presented below in each gateway came as protectors of darkness, in times of darkness—even creating darkness in order to protect the destruction of what is held sacred. I found myself in them. I often feel myself as a guardian of the sacredness of darkness and blackness. In my efforts to protect and guard anything I feel is sacred (including spiritual and religious paths), I can sometimes come across as being just as rageful as the dark mothers in this text who both protect *and* love. And, like these protectors, I come with sword and flowers.

In various cultures across the continents there are deities of darkness and light, night and day, and so forth. The personification of darkness, of the moon, of the light, of the sky and earth, was an ancient way of helping people develop a relationship with what gives birth to everything—to the unseen, to creation, to life. The most popular personified deity in Western culture is God. In a mystical way, God represents all things created from the primordial darkness. Throughout this text, the deities as dark mothers are being used in such a way. They are being offered, not for worship, but for understanding and as points of creating a relational journey in opening to the absence of light.

NAVIGATING THE EIGHT GATEWAYS
IN THE MANDALA OF DARKNESS

In looking deeply into the emergence of wisdom teachings on darkness, I created eight gateways to help navigate this journey of *being in darkness, giving birth in darkness,* and *returning into darkness*—a cyclical walk. In review, the gateways create a mandala of darkness within each one of us, while fostering an integration of wisdom teachings. Each gateway honors and reveals dark mothers as protectors from several traditions so that they may assist you to access the power of darkness within you.

What do I mean by *protectors*? What is the need for protection if darkness is not harmful? To begin with, we are inherently fearful of what we can't see. For this reason, darkness has often been interpreted as dangerous. In ancient times, various animals, deities, gods, goddesses, and spirits were called upon to protect us while experiencing darkness. In the same way, this book offers the dark mothers to protect us with love and concern, but through their fierceness, anger, and rage. Dark mothers and protectors of the sacred darkness are disturbed by ugliness, deceit, dishonesty, mistreatment of others, oppression, corruption, exploitation, abuse, and so on. To disrupt what disturbs them, the wrath of a dark mother as protector comes forth with floods, incurable diseases, rampant plagues, pointless killings, and on and on. Their fierceness is how they protect us in the midst of their love. They cause the experiences we call dark when there are wrongdoings in the world. Their wrath, like the COVID-19 pandemic, has no boundary as far as who is good and who is bad. In essence, protectors of darkness bring more darkness, which in turn brings a wider and unknown landscape to stimulate awareness. Darkness is fierce and makes itself known when we are not aligned with the very earth we walk upon. I believe the great majority of social activists are protectors and dark mothers, no matter their gender. They are fierce protectors of sacred darkness.

The protectors discussed in this book, while mythical in nature, can be used in mending our relationship with darkness and blackness. They are steeped in spiritual traditions that would take a lifetime to engage, so, in still developing my relationships with the deities, I share only the common knowledge of these dark mothers and not the deep-rooted wisdom they hold. I honor those who have lived with and through these dark spirits.

The presentation of the dark mothers here is not meant to take you outside of your spiritual or religious tradition. Remain with what provides a divine presence in your life. Remain with that which guides you. Darkness is inclusive of all things, and therefore the gateways include all our ways of accessing the truth of this life.

Before moving to the gateways of this journey, I want to acknowledge that the dark mothers or protectors presented at some point in spiritual history were gendered in various traditions. But know that in spirit there is no gender. The icon of a dark mother can be any gender or sex, although I acknowledge my cis dominance and female-gendered influence in perspective here, and I also recognize my use of mainstream pronouns and the effect that the polarized English language has on this work. I am actively making efforts to embody nonbinary, gender-fluid wisdom so that it shows in my contributions to the whole, and I seek to include everyone with the hope that all the beautiful ones can find themselves in this writing. For now, the protectors representing the gateways have been gendered as *she, her, he,* and *him,* but in a broad and fluid way. I also acknowledge that the illustrations in this book are accessible only to those with physical sight. Because I believe everyone should have access, I have included as much description as possible. Overall, the most important seeing in this work comes from within.

Lastly, a note about the depictions of the dark mothers in the gateways: These protectors are as I see them, and you may not recognize or resonate with the offered illustrations. I was led to share an African essence of them while still respecting how they are traditionally depicted.

BLESSINGS, GUIDED STILLNESS, AND MEDITATIONS IN EACH GATEWAY

In each gateway, you'll find sections offering blessings, guided stillness practice, and meditations to help you be with the absence of light. The blessings and meditations in this book are best read out loud, in real time or recorded, either by you or by someone else for your benefit. Of course silent meditation is fine, and meditation practices from your own tradition are also welcomed here. Also, meditation for some may mean meditative drumming, singing/chanting, or a silent walk in the woods. Utilize whatever works best for you and dive into this work as honestly and as thoroughly as possible.

- **BLESSINGS.** The word *blessing* is derived from *blōd*, an Old English word that once meant "to redden an altar with blood." In ancient African traditions, there is often a use of blood to activate altars or items on an altar, and Christian rituals include the symbolic drinking of the blood of Christ (as in Holy Communion). In these rituals, the blood serves to connect to what is sacred—to connect to God through the blood of Christ, for example, or to connect the symbols on an altar to the unseen, to spirit. In this book, the blessing is to connect you to the sacred darkness, which is to connect you to the vastness of life—everything is included. In this blessing, poison can be turned to medicine. Darkness helps us find the medicine in the poison. Sometimes medicines are strong. Some poisons need to be rooted out by harsh medicine, and some need a slow, gentle approach. No matter what, the blessing is intended to ease the work with darkness and provide protection with both the medicine and the poison that can present themselves within darkness.

- **GUIDED STILLNESS PRACTICE.** These are not reflective practices, per se. We are using stillness to increase intuition within darkness so that we can access messages or deeper wisdom. The guided stillness sections support you in being with darkness and creating a mandala of an undistorted darkness within you. They are meant to activate the energy of each dark mother and assist in empowering you in darkness. Simply step back and be guided. No thought and no action. Just sit still in a meditative state. Your intuition or even clairvoyance can be cultivated here. Try not to entertain ideas or habits of mind in darkness, but to release them. Again, I suggest having someone read the guided stillness sections to you, or you can record them and play them back so you can simply sit, listen, and go through the process.

  Most importantly, the guided stillness exercises are aligned with the Buddha's Eightfold Path to end suffering (see table 2). The Eightfold Path is not a formula to get rid of all your suffering, but a path to be with the darkness of suffering— how to not suffer inevitable suffering, how to not wait for some idea of light to appear in the unpromised future.

- **MEDITATIONS.** There are meditations of all kinds, from secular to religious. Meditation here is inclusive of all of them—anything that helps to still the mind and disrupts suffering. Meditation does not refer to a particular technique, but more to a way to assist you in meeting darkness, evil, or suffering. It enacts stillness. The "I" in the meditations is inclusive of all people, of all experience. It is a collective "I"—an "I" that has a direct experience of stillness. While *how* you engage with the meditations or blessings is not set in stone, what matters is that you participate in developing an authentic relationship with darkness and blackness.

GATEWAY	DIRECTION	DARK MOTHER	GUIDED STILLNESS	EIGHTFOLD PATH
CLOCKWISE				
First	East	Mahakali/ Daikokutennyo (Indian Hinduism/ Japanese Buddhism)	Wielding the Sword	A Whole View Within the Dark Experience
Second	South	Mama Black Panther (Nature)	Being with a Familiar	Taking the Appropriate Action in Dark Experiences
Third	West	Mama Dantor (Haitian)	Sweetening the Tongue	Sweetness When Speaking Within Dark Experiences
Fourth	North	Mami Wata (Benin, formerly Dahomey)	Wading in the Waters	Intention to Do No Harm Within Dark Experiences
COUNTERCLOCKWISE				
Fifth	North	Mother Ala (Nigerian/ Igbo Odinani)	Asking the Earth	Mindfulness Regarding our Planet
Sixth	West	Papa Damballah (Haitian/West African)	Stoking the Fire	Effort Toward Light as Consciousness and Energy
Seventh	South	Mama Erzulie Je Rouj (Haitian)	Honoring the Demon	Livelihood for the Wellness of All
Eighth	East	Mama Brijit (Haitian)	Listening to the Black Rooster	Meditation as Listening

Table 2. Guided stillness practices and corresponding points on the Buddha's Eightfold Path

You don't have to worry about trying to understand Buddha's teachings of the Eightfold Path. I have highlighted in the chart the essence of the path in relationship to darkness. There are countless books that discuss the Buddha's Eightfold Path (without a relationship to darkness) as a part of the Four Noble Truths, but you may gain a different perspective in the way this path is used in the cessation of suffering within darkness. The most important thing here is to surface what your bones know.

We used to know as human beings how to be with darkness or dark experiences, but we have forgotten over time. We had ways to remain in relationship with darkness and with one another while experiencing collective darkness. We participated in ceremonies that showed us how to invoke our true nature of lovingkindness, compassion, sympathetic joy, and equanimity, but our intellect—rooted in aggression and busyness (the ways of our country)—has taken center stage in our lives. The mandala of darkness and the Eight Gateways' use of the attributes of the dark mother deities in relationship to Buddha's Eightfold Path is intended to help you rediscover this ancient knowing for being with the absence of light.

When you step into the mandala of darkness through the gateways, you break the surface of things that have obstructed your view of darkness. You disrupt the constant yearning for peace and light. You sit still in the darkness and listen for what is needed. If you have peace, then what? If you have light, then what? How do we navigate the constant storms of life?

The Eight Gateways are dead on the written page until you experience them. Engage the blessings, the guided stillness exercises, and the meditations as a way to embody what is being taught. If you find yourself confused or unable to hold it all in your mind, let go of this exploration as an intellectual process.

We are all born. Along the way, the hope is that we learn not only to speak of our suffering but to understand it. In other words, we eventually begin to use the suffering to surface wisdom and compassion from the darkness—not from our minds but from just being. We begin to ask questions and make the quest of life right where we are. We already live and will continue to live in the deep woods of darkness.

Our quest for well-being is not for us only but for our families and communities that are in despair. The wilderness of our lives is a place in which we can recover from being discombobulated in our displacement from the things we once knew as human beings before so-called progress. Many people meditate without understanding that it is not a tool to enforce calmness. The promise of meditation is that we become mediums for the wisdom found in darkness and dark experiences. Mediumship is indigenous to our nature.

The point is not to reenergize the suffering while engaging the mandala but to settle upon suffering as if it were a pillow made of soft earth and we were lying awake in the dark—feeling expansive, fierce, and capable in the dark. Also, we are not on a quest in life to gain a vision here but on a quest in which a vision of life surfaces on its own. It emerges from where it has always been.

The transformative process begins with your own truth of suffering. You may have read many books and talked to many teachers, and yet you still struggle with this life, which is to struggle with darkness. If we can't end inevitable suffering, we certainly can end the struggling with it. Few books or teachers have advised us to stay in this darkness. The Eightfold Path itself is often thought of as a path to end suffering and darkness. But I see it as an ancient path to *be with* suffering and darkness.

In these gateways we are looking into darkness, not for light, but for what darkness has to reveal. The moment we met with our first pain and then experienced suffering, we were initiated into darkness. We are initiated at birth, and eventually we experience personal and collective trauma—collective darkness—in the hope that we can collectively see and know. Our work is not only healing the woundedness but walking with monsters until the monsters lose their teeth and therefore their grip on us.

Another important reminder: In making the mandala of darkness within ourselves, we are not calling in the dark mothers, nor are we learning the Buddhist way to live. Instead, we are utilizing the *attributes* of the deities and the *essence* of the Eightfold Path. Let's keep going.

INSTRUCTIONS FOR GUIDED STILLNESS SECTIONS AND CREATING THE MANDALA OF DARKNESS WITHIN

To prepare for the guided stillness practices of each gate, please create a sacred space in your house in which you will sit each time. It's best to be seated on the ground or the floor. If you need a stool or chair, that's fine, but try to sit as close to the ground as possible. You might want to use a special seat or cloth to put on the floor for this journey. On the ground, you are connecting to earth, to mother, which means you're connecting to yourself through the earth as ancestor. Wherever and whatever you choose to sit upon, consider this spot your dharma seat. Coming from Sanskrit, *dharma* is not only a Buddhist term meaning "teachings." It is an ancient word that predates the Buddha, and it represents the inherent universal truth of all things and beings. Therefore, your dharma seat is where there will be an exchange between you and inconceivable darkness.

You will place your dharma seat in the direction of the gateway prescribed—east, south, west, north. These directions create a simple mandala as you first move clockwise and then counterclockwise. The clockwise (outer ring) route is meant to introduce you to the ancestors, give thanks, share, and ask for insight. In going clockwise through the first four gates, you will focus on more personal experiences of suffering in dark times. Counterclockwise (inner ring, the last four gates), the focus is more on the collective experiences of dark times. In the counterclockwise movement, you go back and gather the wisdom of the ancestors. Ancestors are those who have come before us, including the earth and its trees, water, stars, sun, moon, et cetera. Ancestors can include your bloodline from your family of origin, the lineage of your chosen spiritual path, or any unspecified ancestors who know you even if you don't know them. Ancestors can also include animals other than humans. Anything or anyone who has come before you is what has sustained you and brought you to this moment.

As you sit on your dharma seat, no candles, incense, or statues are necessary. Quiet is key. When you are quiet and still, you will be able to fully experience darkness. Sit with your buttocks or feet on the ground, your body alert, with eyes open or closed. The point is to prepare yourself to receive—not from me as the author, but from the darkness.

MINDSET FOR ENTERING
THE GATEWAYS

In creating the mandala of darkness within you, you turn from striving toward a light that is imagined or manufactured. Instead, turn toward darkness and remain in it. Doing so, we begin to see that our very life is dark, unknown, and often troubled. I realize that I am repeating myself here, but know that we have lived with darkness since birth and will continue to until death. Darkness is a great mystery, so we are that mystery, because we have descended from darkness. We are here to engage life in the vastness of the troubled waters of darkness.

An important note before creating the mandala: At any time, if you find you need help and support, please get assistance from a healing professional, mentor, spiritual teacher, medicine person, or clergy member. Also keep in mind that it is fine to do this work in community as well, as long as you can share the experience of this mandala.

The mandala is designed for you to move in the directions provided. Entering the gateway that you favor before completing the cycle at least once is to continue having preferences that may lead to confusion. After you have completed the Eight Gateway mandala as prescribed, then perhaps you can enter the gateway that assisted you best without going through the preceding gateways first.

Opening to darkness will help you discover what light truly is—not your light, not mine, not a color, not even necessarily a brightness, but more of an awareness that exists outside of our thinking. Through these gateways, perhaps the journey will help you:

- Experience the wonders of life that can only flourish in the dark

- Discover a collective doorway to healing and deep transformation

- Awaken to the illusory nature of light versus dark

- Illuminate false perceptions and beliefs of darkness

- Heal the fear and anxiety around darkness and blackness

Maybe you are ready. Maybe not. Maybe you've been here before. Either way, as we enter this cyclical path, know that these gateways reside within the rageful *and* loving heart. We are taking a walk around a mandala of our profound inner and outer lives. Let's begin the walk through the eight gates with this prayer-poem I penned after the death of George Floyd at the hands of police.

> Darkness is asking to be loved
> When we have lost the tiny sense of peace we
>   created for ourselves. Our composure, an idea
>   long gone, reflected in the grinding of teeth and
>   locked jaws, shock hidden beneath fear.
> Holding shoulders up to meditate while sliding off—
> I invite you to fall down on the earth.
>
> Come down here and smell the sweat of terror on your
>   skin, overpowering the scent of agarwood. Come
>   down on all fours and greet the darkness that reeks
>   of death, reaches out its desperate hand, and asks
>   to be loved as much as we love the light it gives.
>
> Breathe for those gasping for air.
>
> Come down here on this earth. Each scream a bell that
>   never stops ringing. Bury your face in the mud of
>   this intimate place, in shared disease and tragedy.

If you have nothing to say, now is the time for the deeper
    silence honed that does not apologize or seek something
    kind to say. And yet the deeper silence is not quiet. It
    whispers in the dark and wakes you from the nightmare.

Come down here and be still on the earth. Let
    loose shame, rage, guilt, grief, pain, and make
    a river of it, or a mountain, or an ocean.

Come down here. Catch the love poems hidden in
    the shouting, watch the unfolding of the seasons
    from the ground, look up at the sky. And when it
    hurts from being down here so long, roll over and
    see what you couldn't see from the other side.

Breathe out loud. No particular posture needed.

Fall down onto the earth. Fall off your soft cushions.
    Come down here. Come down here, where the
    only lullaby tonight will be the sound of your
    heart drumming the songs you were born with.

PART 2

FIRST GATEWAY

THE NATURE OF DARKNESS

Mahakali/Daikokutennyo

The wrathful dakini Troma Nagmo (Krodha Kali), a primary deity of the Buddhist Nyingma Chöd practice, is Mahakali. Daikokutennyo is the expression of Mahakali in Japanese Buddhism. Mahakali—or Kali, as she is known—is the fierce black Hindu goddess of destruction. Kali is so fierce, she slices through all the illusions that move us in destructive ways, and she ultimately destroys the world when and where it needs destroying. In this way, her energy is much like that of Manjushri Bodhisattva, a statue who sits, instead of Buddha, in the meditation hall of most Zen centers. Like Manjushri, Mahakali uses her sword to cut away from our heart and mind that which is not in alignment with the well-being of all.

Mahakali can represent the cutting away of ignorance, such as that experienced regarding darkness, including any oppressions based on darkness. In other depictions, Kali stands on the body of Shiva to symbolize her fierce devotion to the protection of life, especially the lives of women and children. Through women, she is protecting the integrity of humanity.

Mahakali carries the snakes for humanity's protection and inevitable transformation. The skulls around her neck in my image are not so much a banner of who she has killed; rather, they represent the ignorance and misdirection within human beings. The skulls can represent awakening here, too. She reveals the impermanence of all things, including what we fear and hate.

Mahakali will destroy only what needs to be destroyed in us. She is a dark mother of this earth and is capable of discerning the nature of reality in terms of how we are conditioned as human beings. She is not outside of us. We are all fierce in a purposeful way if we allow it. And this fierceness can be used in experiences of darkness. Let's enter this first gateway in the east with Mahakali as embodied darkness that we experienced in the wombs of our mothers.

In this first gateway we are beginning to open and accept darkness into our lives. We are standing with the fierceness of Mahakali and gathering the skulls of things destroyed for the growth of humanity. We are transforming in the midst of all destruction around us. In order to do such, there is a need to understand the nature of darkness. This isn't a request for you to stay with what feels bad. It is an invitation to see into darkness and to transform negative feelings about our dark experiences and see the true nature of darkness.

Imagine Mahakali looking with you, no matter who you are, at leftover pieces from things that needed to be destroyed for the sake of well-being—personal and collective. To destroy, obliterate, disintegrate anything can be seen as dark action. But these actions by Mahakali are meant to reconnect us to fierce aspects of ourselves that we often trade in for kinder versions, whereas both exist. The authentic nature of darkness is to destroy and transform, and therefore we fear it, even to the point of becoming terrorized. The disconnection from darkness creates fear and a distorted view of it within our hearts and minds. We have been severed from darkness because the kind of destruction we see with Mahakali energy has been deemed wrong. Yet this work is not dressing up darkness or making it sweet to swallow. It is not making it presentable or putting language to it so that the world accepts it. It is opening to all that darkness gives and changes, whether desired or not. In opening to darkness, we can become more acquainted with the nature of not only the harshness of darkness but also the sweetness of it.

I noticed that much of what has been written on darkness in all disciplines (religion, spirituality, psychology, sociology, and so forth) has come from those not embodied in dark skin. Many of the authors have not had to contend with articulating the experience of living in a dark body in relationship with darkness in its broader existence. In embracing Mahakali, I was embracing myself not only in energy but in body as well. As mentioned earlier, it was difficult for me to distinguish between darkness as a universal experience and my personal experience of living in a dark-skinned body. Both are so interconnected that there is no line dividing the two. The sorrow, grief, pain, *and* liberating aspects of both being black and experiencing darkness are one. Living in a dark body required inviting darkness into my life and experiencing the warriorship of Mahakali in my life. None of us can escape darkness, whether we are embodied with dark faces or not. In feeling Mahakali's face as my own, snarled and black, it was important for my survival to reclaim the purity of darkness. It was also important to note that darkness and blackness, even in a dark body, remain a universal experience regardless of the color of one's skin. What is different from one person to the next is the lived experience of darkness, which may vary depending on heritage, culture, class, gender, and so on. I may carry a sword to protect the sanctity of humanity by slicing through the idea that one kind of person is more superior, or inferior, than another. At the same time, another person may carry it to protect something from their life experience.

We have unique insights into the realm of darkness: unbearable, powerful, universal, ancestral, and cosmic. Writing the teachings here was an act of compassion. It came from pain and the understanding that every human being experiences such pain. It came from tears and from not knowing what it meant to live in darkness. This writing is an evolution that was not only personal but a collective tuning into darkness as a known and unknown experience of life. Ultimately, creating a willingness among many to learn how to be with dark times together.

We don't know how to be *with* and *in* darkness while carrying the sword of Mahakali. We slice without investigation, or we unconsciously support in countless ways, turning away or demonizing the dark across various dimensions of life: culture, tradition, religion, and racial embodiment. The demonizing of darkness means to strip it of its essential human potential to disrupt and to renew. From a place of horror, darkness isn't redeemable. Separated from the universal human and spiritual experience, it creates fear and oppression while uplifting manufactured light, lightness, or light supremacy. For this reason, it is important, even for those of us who love darkness, to examine ourselves in relationship to darkness—to that which is destructive, earth-shattering, and unbearable. Is there a willingness to listen to what darkness is asking of us in its presence? What do dark experiences push us to do personally and collectively? How does darkness serve our lives? We are walking together every day in darkness. It is here *for* us. And all of these questions can be used to explore our relationships to dark experiences (collective and personal), dark people, and dark matter.

Before moving on, take some time to examine your own heart and mind. Notice your response to the appearance of darkness and blackness (as flesh, as fur on an animal, as paint, as a crayon, as the color of someone's eyes or hair). I am asking this of all people whether you are embodied in dark skin or not, getting at the root of what you might eliminate of physical or nonphysical darkness without investigation.

Oneness of Darkness and Blackness

In my experience as black skinned, the imperative to embody and embrace darkness has always seemed obvious. But I have also found it difficult, because opening to darkness was complex, existential, and multidimensional. In feeling the challenges of embracing and living in darkness and blackness, I gravitated toward spirituality looking for light, looking for awareness. In deep meditation, rituals, and ceremonies that began in my late teens and lasted over many years, I began to see the evolution of embodied blackness—that it wasn't static—and I understood that everyone was continually experiencing darkness in some way. It was not the darkness of appearance necessarily, but a darkness that exists as itself in the scheme of life.

When I dropped all the adjectives around darkness (not "positive," not "negative," not "hard"), darkness and blackness began to exist together with profound characteristics and ways of expression within life. Blackness and darkness were beyond me. I realized that the nature of *both as one* created a broader view of being black and of living in the midst of dark experiences. In realizing the oneness of darkness and blackness, I discovered blackness wasn't this tight existence because it was at one with darkness. So when I say "blackness," I know it to be at one with darkness, and darkness at one with blackness. We know that Mahakali is usually imaged as black, and yet it is not the same blackness conceived during the centuries of enslavement of Africans. It is a blackness perceived in Hinduism.

Perhaps we can all arrive at the same broad view by entering at the door of darkness in our lives and come to see blackness, to see the oneness, and to discover the existential nature of dark and black. Some of us may be physically black, but that is only one aspect of blackness. Blackness is of the greater darkness.

In this willingness to open the experience of blackness into darkness, I noticed the oppressive framing, descriptions, and misinterpretations of blackness began to fall away, and I experienced both darkness and blackness as ever evolving. *Both as one* is indescribable, formless, and without comprehension with our small minds. This darkness has never been in my control to turn off and on, to be fixed by therapy or religion. There was no more destruction necessary, no more trying to slay the beast of oppression, no more skulls to gather. This sense of an unfixed darkness became a welcomed expression of life and not something that intrudes upon all that is good and light. In this welcome state, I began to embrace darkness as a compassionate act toward all that was dark in my life, to see darkness in all of its glorious vastness. I had compassion for the fear I felt and for not knowing that the experience of darkness in a dark body was a path in itself of embracing life.

Darkness is neither negative nor positive. We can't add to or take away anything from such a magnificent existence as darkness. In this life, we simply face our fear of experiences with darkness, dark things, and dark people, caused by distortions and disconnection from one another.

The Spirituality of Darkness and Blackness

Darkness and blackness are paths of spirit experienced in the body. In many spiritual traditions the body is considered to be part of the earth if not the earth itself. We think of soil as dark and rich—the ground upon which we stand. The indigenous world is the earth. Because of this, cultures around the world use drums to match the heartbeat of the earth and celebrate deities or archetypes that represent the energy of the dark mother or Mother Earth. These deities are not owned by any culture— they are always of the earth. Mahakali, as a dark mother, is of the earth. Miranda Shaw, the scholar and tantric Buddhist practitioner, once said, "Mahakali will feed her devotees with her own body, because her own body is the earth itself."[4] It is her way of giving sustenance in the dark, as we are fed in our mother's womb. In essence, Mahakali represents us and the darkness within our lives, but in a spiritual sense.

Open land, a forest, the sky, and the deep ocean are physical representations of our vast darkness. Being willing to open to darkness is to be willing to open to unknown dimensions of life, creating the vastness that nature presents. We are the dark waters and the dark earth. To fear darkness and avoid it is to turn against ourselves. When we turn against ourselves, darkness intensifies and is turbulent (personally and collectively).

At a writers' gathering in the woods near Puget Sound in Washington State, I always managed to leave our shared dinner early enough to get to my cabin before nightfall. Oftentimes, I declined an invitation to stay in the living room and chat later into the night because I wasn't at the gathering to chat; I was there to write. Everyone was impressed with my diligence. But I'd also leave dinner early, because—at that time in my life—I was afraid to walk alone in the dark. Though part of the retreat was to be together as writers, the others hung out while I scurried to my cabin.

One night I decided to make a phone call on the landline to a close friend. I was on the phone for a good while. I heard the women writers in the other room laughing and talking. I thought to join them after my call, but the conversation on the phone went longer than expected. When I was done, I noticed it was quiet in the living room and it was dark outside. I went to check the room, hoping someone was there to walk with me at least down the main road. I would have to go the rest of the way by myself, as the cabins were spread throughout the land. My heart sank when I saw that the living room was empty and the lights were out.

I had left my flashlight in my cabin, too, because I didn't expect to need one. I decided to walk as fast as I could back to my cabin, as if walking fast in the dark would enable me to avoid any tragedy that might happen along the way. But trouble can happen in seconds.

There was absolutely no light. The new moon was a sliver. I couldn't see my hands or feet. I could only feel my body moving like a cartoon character. I heard rustling in the bushes, and of course that speeded things up. I imagined that the sounds I heard were bears or wolves, neither of which lived in that part of the wilderness. But I walked even faster and ran right into a huge cedar tree. I hit my head and stumbled and nearly passed out. I cursed quietly. I was harshly reminded there was a tree at the fork in the road. I had missed my turn by less than a foot. I backed up and veered left of the tree so that my feet could find the correct path. I couldn't see in the dark, but I knew my cabin was about twenty feet left of the tree. In the end, I was happy there was a tree to stop me. I would have walked so deep into the forest that I would have had to wait out there until morning.

In the forest, I was disconnected from earth and from myself as the dark earth. I didn't know how to walk with the darkness that is ever present—that darkness was within me even in daylight. The walk in the dark was an opportunity to see myself, to greet the jackrabbit in me that was absent in the big city's overly lit streets. Or was that true? Was I generally afraid of the unseen?

Do you find yourself running from what you can't see? Take a moment to see the animal in you that runs, the natural instinct to protect yourself. To keep yourself alive. But is there a deeper situation and more pervasive way in which you avoid conflict and chaos in an effort to have peace? Do you speed walk through dark times? When sensing darkness, what is it that you are afraid of? Spend some time here breathing in those times you were paralyzed by darkness, including dark experiences, things, and people.

Becoming lost in the forest and seeing the depth of fear brought an experience of compassion for the animal in me and for the intense need to survive. I was always running in life, with a constant need to save myself. Are you constantly ensuring your own safety before the darkness appears in your life? Although we encounter dark times in many ways, our survival instinct runs high, and we are not sure what we are running from. At the same time, we are not sure if we have what we need to survive darkness. Yet it is possible to discover what we need if we are willing to investigate dark experiences, to study darkness beyond indoctrination, and to suspend for a moment the notions of darkness as shadowy, bad, or negative. In my willingness to investigate such in my own life, I began a process of opening to an evolutionary blackness—one that was not only of history but of the moment. I was both fearful and ready. Investigation, exploration, examination of one's fear of dark experiences is the first act in accepting the absence of light.

Are you willing to investigate what you call dark? What ways can you begin to see into the spirituality of darkness? You can't escape darkness or the harsh realities of life, just as I couldn't escape that walk alone at the writers' retreat. Physical darkness and intangible darkness had always been there. They will be in my life forever. If darkness is there always, then it is life. To greet the dark and receive it is to be relieved of being haunted by it.

A willingness to be in the dark is a willingness to see darkness in its highest and most sacred expression as being in everything. Destruction is in everything. Being willing to welcome the unknown leads to a liberated darkness—one not encumbered by imposed perceptions or fear and disdain.

The dark in our lives is ever evolving and interdependent with what is happening in the moment. In essence, it is dynamic and shape-shifting, meaning it can present in almost any form. Mahakali (or Daikokutennyo) is both a fierce and a serene form of darkness and blackness. Even with skulls and sword, Mahakali is still and silent. The forest in which the writers' retreat took place was wild and tame, pleasant and unpleasant. Life in a dark body for me is both harsh and profound. Not knowing what life is bringing from the darkness can be frightening and intriguing. The nature of dark experiences rattles everything loose so that we can see also that the serenity we desire is present. Without the rattling, our suffering is fixed.

Over time, when fear emerged from me in the physical darkness of the woods, like walking at night alone at the retreat center, I began to see my body blending in. Disappearing into nothingness, disappearing into the absence of light. Like dropping into an existence without space and time. When it comes to feeling the sense of folding into blackness, skin color doesn't matter. We have all come through the womb of our mothers as far as we know. While the womb serves the process of gestation after the planting of seeds, it is our first home on earth. It may not have been a pleasant home. It may have been a home of turmoil, illness, grief. We don't often talk about the womb as a place of disruption. And we rarely see or acknowledge that the dark womb was also born of darkness. In opening to the dark of our lives, we are reaching back into the source of life, the womb. When I am in the woods at night I reach back into the darkness my body knows from being in the womb. Yet it is an unknown source that can create fear. With the unknown, I take a breath. I investigate the story in my head that blocks my heart from opening.

What is your story around the dark things in life? How does that story create fear or terror? Can you find a place to be empowered in it? Can you let go of searching for serenity and allow the dark to guide you there?

Darkness as Source: Mother and Womb

If we contemplate darkness of the womb, a home we may not remember, then the feelings of eeriness, evil, or shadow that we place on what's dark may begin to fade. As far as we know, the pathway of the womb into life could be the same pathway to death, making the dark womb the home of birth and death, both of which we know little about. While we can't literally reenter the womb (and some of us would neither need nor want to), it would be an act of compassion to reflect upon our relationship to the archetype of the dark mother, as well as on our own mother in relationship to darkness. Perhaps we can take a look at *mother* in her divine state—disruptive and sublime.

The womb provided warmth, moisture, blood, water, air, food, and other substances to grow flesh, hair, and muscles. To consider the womb as source of darkness, as source of life, is a way to open to the darkness that birthed us—a darkness that could be abundant, tragic, and cosmic.

For many, if not all, our relationship to mother is troubled, even though her womb provided for us. In essence, we have our own personal dark mothers who were, or are, wrathful in their protection of their children. Human conditioning and the social pressures put upon mothers also lead to dark experiences that encourage many of us to decide that darkness is to be avoided at all costs.

I've often said that my own mother rotated like our planet—from light to dark, rough to smooth; from giving to not being able to give after so much was being taken from her by her family and the world. She was wrathful and generous. When we think of our mothers, many of us might feel as though we have been born to Mahakali. But she would be a Mahakali as mother *and* womb who can provide soul, spirit, and consciousness in the aggressive, wrathful darkness—raw energy. Our nonphysical aspects of our lives originate from the darkness as much as the physical ones. Our relationship with our mothers can be considered a physical relationship to darkness, and perhaps the reason many of us struggle with our mothers is because we struggle with darkness and have imposed our disdain and fear of darkness upon our mothers, upon women in general, and upon the appearance of the feminine despite gender.

To establish a relationship with the womb, if only in our imaginations, is to open to darkness as life-giving. It would be a compassionate act to reenter a relationship with darkness—as mother, as creator, as a birthplace of us all. Even if that mother, that darkness, is Mahakali, both wild and serene, with sword and skulls.

To help you establish a relationship to darkness and see darkness as life-giving, read or chant the following words out loud:

In the beginning, the dark water of the womb was home.
Without ears, eyes, a nose, a tongue, without light, there was still
sight, smell, sound, taste, and touch.
We descended in birth from the great mystery of the dark,
making us rich and full with the forever unknown.

When darkness is palpable and driving you insane, remember you are being offered another birthplace or another chance to be born—or to die if needed.

Darkness is living and life-giving. It turns us inward to the mysteries that are meant, not to be solved, but still to be considered. In our unsettled places with darkness, we may attempt to oppress, ignore, or neglect it in an effort to control the amount of darkness we comfortably want to experience. At the same time, we know there is no way to control darkness as much as we would like to. We want to be comfortable in this life. But to be always comfortable is to not be alive. We are dead in constant comfort. And if we are dead, we are not sure that we are resting in peace and power or resting in the same struggle and anxiousness of life. We are all of darkness and blackness in the same way we are of God, so to speak. Our dark lives are divinity itself.

Darkness as Divine

Darkness is often viewed as not only absent of color but absent of the divine, absent of goodness, absent of God. Is Mahakali divine in her snarl, her growl, her aggression? Is she not also empowering the feminine, the serene and sublime? In her darkness is a place of divinity, the location where many gods and goddesses dwell. Her dark intervention of destruction on behalf of humanity in the form of tragedies, pandemics, wars, or senseless killings is a mark of her divine presence in our lives. She says, "Cease all that is not aligned with the earth and with well-being, or there will be more destruction."

The Black Angel oracle cards that I published many years ago came to me in a lucid dream. They are of this dark and black divinity, black angels, dark mothers—of darkness, of God, of creation. They were a dark intervention. They arrived at the darkest and most transformative time of my life. I have never written about the darkness of the oracle, although a medium helped me see the woundedness that scented them. The fragrance of pain drew the wounded to the work of divining in the midst of our suffering. Many folks—including black women for whom the cards were gifted at the inception—were frightened of the cards. They even labeled the cards demonic. One black woman asked me, "Why do those angels have to be black?" Her nose was turned up—yes, turned up at blackness. I asked her, "What color should they be?" She didn't answer. Some feared that using the cards would be to hold court with the devil, which would harm them or even bring death. When we perceive darkness through the eyes and hearts of those who have hated darkness, we hate darkness, too. And we grow to hate dark experiences, not knowing that we are hating life itself.

The word *black* in the Black Angel cards expresses the darkness—the location of divinity in which an angel comes into being. When I divine with the cards, the messages come from the darkness of suffering. I cannot see where they are coming from with my mind. I trust that the messages come from the dark, from the ancestors. I am just as in awe at the truth of the messages when I divine for others. The dark angels inside the darkness of the oracle are there to slay the distortions and oppression around darkness and blackness in our society and to reclaim the purity of darkness for the sake of saving many from further suffering. I knew this when the oracle was delivered. I even said out loud, "Ancestors, this is too big of a job for me." The negativity placed on blackness and the color black is as ancient as humanity. Why should I be chosen to slay this terrible dragon? And I knew I was not the only one with this mission. But it isn't until now that I am able to write about the depth of consciousness surrounding the oracle and say that the oracle itself had been laid inside me. That I was the oracle. But it felt too bold to walk in the world claiming to be an oracle. So I placed the medicine in a book, on art, on cards to be shuffled. I took the responsibility of being an oracle off me so that the Mahakali energy within the pages wouldn't be seen as *me* cutting off the heads of those who were coming for healing (even though their heads needed cutting off).

This writing is an extension of the oracle, of teachings in the dark, of dark mothers, of dark pain and suffering. And my relationship with my own mother who gave birth to me was not as much a relationship of *mother and daughter* but one of *dark mother to dark daughter*. My mother was never meant to bake cookies, like the mothers I saw on TV while growing up. She was to lead me into the depth of darkness of life that I knew but feared.

I eventually came to consider each archetype in the oracle deck as a divine mother. All dark mothers are of divine darkness, of God, or of that which creates and protects life. The late Ntozake Shange, the renowned poet and playwright, conveyed the dark divine in her acclaimed work *for colored girls who have considered suicide / when the rainbow is enuf*:

> Through my tears
> I found god in myself

This Obie Award–winning choreopoem, one of the first major plays by a black woman in our country since *A Raisin in the Sun* by the late Lorraine Hansberry, ran on Broadway from 1976 to 1977. It was an artistic expression—through poetry, dance, and song—of darkness as sacred, yet often exploited, destroyed, or eliminated. Shange invited black women to consider a spirituality of darkness in the midst of the dark experiences of being black. It brought the insurmountable pain of being dark into the realm of God and divinity. The play presents seven black women dressed in the colors of the rainbow, each expressing their dark experiences of life.

I was fortunate enough to see the play when it arrived fresh from New York to Berkeley and Los Angeles, California. I witnessed each woman on stage carrying the dark mother essence in each move, and in each voice I heard a definitive welcoming of their experience of their rage misunderstood and their love unseen because of their rage. To find God in these black women's experiences of abortion, rape, sex, joy, and grief was to know a dark life as divine. To find God in oneself was not an acclamation of the ego—not a holier-than-thou pronouncement. In watching this profound play in a theater filled mostly with black women, my bones said, *We are celebrating being born in darkness*.

All human beings, despite their skin color, are divined by darkness and then born of darkness, born of the dark wombs of our mothers and the dark wombs of all mothers long before our time. Opening to darkness is opening to this universal truth. To turn away from this truth is to turn away from the source of all life.

The dark mother may show up anywhere during our suffering. Once while sitting in a sesshin, a seven-day Zen retreat, I opened my eyes to keep from falling asleep. On the wall in front of me, I saw an image that wasn't really there—a mother cradling her child. It was a simple image created by the lines in the wall. It came and disappeared and returned. I stayed awake for the rest of the meditation watching the mother and child who were on the wall and yet not on the wall, until the bell rang to end the session. I hurried (as much as one can in Zen robes) to my room. I sat down and drew the image. In my journey of opening to darkness, the mother and child appeared as I was suffering in the dark meditation hall. The image of the mother could have been any of the dark mothers from any divine pantheon of goddesses who protect children who are suffering from what they face in the world. The image itself came from darkness—the same darkness I was sitting in and opening.

What if darkness came to reveal the divinity in your life? It is an unknown divinity, because you are discovering yourself as divine. Take some time right now to consider darkness as divine presence. Breathe into the possibilities. Is it possible that the dark experiences are revealing you as God or a life-giving presence?

Even though the character in Shange's play claims the divinity of God in herself as a black woman, the larger play is experienced as a ceremony in which God surfaces from the darkness of all, despite race and gender. God is real *and* a metaphor affirming a historical and theological reality for the divine that is born of darkness. For me, in the wall of the zendo, the divine intervention of a mother and child was significant, given one of the core teachings of the Buddha is to feel for others the love a mother might feel for her only child. But then again, darkness is not mother alone. Darkness is not womb alone. Darkness is not me. Although mother, womb, and me are all embodied darkness.

We embody the dark between sunset and sunrise. Twilight is considered in many traditions around the world as the time in which the veil is thin between the relative and spirit worlds. It is a time to stop, reflect, pray, or meditate. It is when darkness intervenes in our lives and shakes us awake. In the early morning hours (known as the *bewitching* or *witching* hours), it is said that magic is done to us, in us, and around us. There are many who can divine in this darkness and conjure protection.

What messages come through you when darkness arrives? If dark experiences arise with such intensity, could you use them to enhance your view of life? Could you use the loss, the craziness, and the fearful things that come to you in the dark? Is there a divinity or sacredness in heavy darkness?

Darkness in its divinity is good fortune. Whenever I'd tell them about the darkness in my life, my first teachers in the Nichiren Buddhist tradition would always congratulate me. At first it would make me angry. I needed them to agree with how bad it was to be miserable in the darkness. Every week, month, and year I would complain of my misfortunes. It took years before I realized the misfortune of darkness was good fortune, too, as a timeless gestation and awakening for my life. Darkness was here to stay. It was my view of it as troublesome that caused suffering. I grew to love dark experiences as divine experiences. I did not use darkness to gain more knowledge or gain some idea of wisdom. I let darkness use me. In honoring darkness, I also congratulate aspirants when they speak of their suffering. *We are fortunate that darkness exists.* That's what my Nichiren Buddhist teachers were saying when they congratulated me. And even today I still cry, scream, and emote in the darkness, asking to be loved and attended to. It's a relationship I can never divorce, so I welcome it and allow the suffering to show me, teach me.

A relationship with darkness is not for pleasure or happiness. Yes, I enjoy a dark room as the sun sets. There is no suffering. But what I speak of here is a darkness that reveals itself over and over, in painful ways, until it gets what it wants from us. A collective opening to darkness is crucial to love.

Mantras Used for Collective Openings to Darkness

Mantra is a Sanskrit word comprised of the root words *manas* ("mind" or "to think") and *tra* ("vehicle"). A mantra can be an affirmation, a rallying call to the soul, or simply a set of sounds without meaning that concentrate the mind and purify it of thoughts that lead to suffering. In the use of the mantra, the body is activated along with the consciousness that is being called upon in the mantra.

In reflecting upon opening to blackness and darkness, I considered the mantras regarding blackness from a historical collective of black people. The mantra "Black Lives Matter" brought a love movement into the world through black women warriors Alicia Garza, Patrisse Cullors, and Opal Tometi. Their mantra came from an old cry: "Black is Beautiful." It came from James Brown's "Say It Loud—I'm Black and I'm Proud." From janitors on strike during the civil rights movement: "I Am a Man." From Sojourner Truth's "Ain't I a Woman?" From Jill Scott's song "Golden," in which the mantra is to live one's life "like it's golden"—*a golden black life.*

The mantras honoring black people come from the same place as the cries of Kuan Yin, the bodhisattva of compassion. The mantras of awakening come from the darkness of suffering, from collective assault upon the soul, spirit, and consciousness. There has been a long-standing cry for dignity by black people and other marginalized groups. It is a cry for the return of love given despite acts of hatred for centuries. The calls are from the deep caves where many bones of those marginalized were left without honor. Loud chanting is not hatred. It is rage for all that has gone against the well-being of humanity. Dark people, along with others who could see, have carried the rich, dark energy of the dark mother deities from all over the world—to guard the integrity of humanity by destroying, as Mahakali would, those things that harm living beings. This destruction of ignorance can come through a collective mantra.

"Black Lives Matter" was the first chant of a collective dark body that crossed racial color lines. When others joined in the mantra, we, collectively, opened to darkness and blackness—not just black people but many others. It was the beginning of opening and seeing darkness in the world as an interrelated experience among all humans, whether it was received that way or not.

The experience of the collective mantra "Black Lives Matter" began a process to reclaim the universal purity of darkness, to erase the filth and horridness imposed upon it. When darkness appears, it is asking to be loved as much as we love the perceived light we believe it brings. Many misunderstood the "Black Lives Matter" mantra and thought it was a mantra of hatred against whites. They didn't know that the mantra included them as human beings who are part of the greater darkness and blackness in life. At the extreme, this misunderstanding fueled a white people's power movement based on hatred, unlike the black power movement, which is based on ending hatred. But it must be realized that collective mantras of hatred come from the same darkness as mantras of love. Since we do not know what is being born of darkness, it is difficult for many to open to it because of our experiences of injury and harm. But what is being born is being born no matter what. Dark events in our lives are calling for our attention and engagement. A collective opening to darkness, regardless of what it delivers, is expanded awakening and an opportunity to reveal a path for an ascended humanity.

Is there anything that calls your soul to darkness? What words would you use to affirm or honor darkness? Can those words be used to create a mantra of your own? Maybe it is not a mantra but a poetic rendition, song, dance, or drum rhythm that rises when you hear darkness calling your attention.

It takes courage to open to darkness, to open to destruction. I tried to destroy that which I thought was wrong, without any notion that the destruction was misplaced—not done in guardianship of humanity. The destruction came from wounding, not from protecting essential darkness and blackness. Eventually, I relinquished my intangible weapons and traded them for a pen and paper to write down what I couldn't say out loud. In order to write, I had to dwell in darkness, witness it, breathe it in, wonder about it, fear its potency, and, at times, be ashamed of misinterpreted darkness and blackness in the midst of exhalting whiteness and lightness.

When we become aware of darkness, we are charged with finding ways to dwell in it, hopefully without harm. When darkness is seen and felt, it teaches us to dwell with life, with both the harshness and the softness of it. The awareness of darkness is an indication of being in the experience of expansion and renewal. It is a time when we can enact transformation.

Opening to darkness is a call to turn, like the earth that you are, on your axis into darkness and allow it to exist as it is, as an assistant to awakening. Please take the time now to activate the mandala in you based on Mahakali's energy of fierceness. Remember, if you find the need for help and support, please get assistance from a healing professional, a mentor, or a clergy person. It is fine to do this work in community as well. It is best done in community with a seasoned facilitator of healing circles.

Let's take the first step in creating our mandala of darkness within.

GUIDED STILLNESS ONE

Wielding the Sword
Working with Mahakali's Sword
East Direction
A Whole View Within the Dark Experience

Take your dharma seat in a quiet space in the east direction. Take a deep breath and release it slowly. Very slowly. Repeat several times. Then breathe in your own rhythm.

Read the blessing as if someone like myself is blessing you on your journey.

Blessing

May the great darkness still your mind and body.
Let it reveal what needs to be revealed in the disturbances of your life.
May what needs to be destroyed in darkness be destroyed for the sake of awakening.

Be well and stay well in darkness all the days of your life. Stop and breathe. Close your eyes.

Guided Stillness

What darkness are you suffering from in this moment? Pause. Is it a loss, a relationship struggle, an illness, a life transition, or something else?

You are still breathing in and out. Say to yourself regarding your struggle, "This is renewal taking place." Say, "This is awakening taking place."

Now is the time for honesty. Find two or three words that describe what you are suffering. If you have more, that is fine.

Lay these words mentally on an imagined carving table. Look over these words. Have they contributed to you being weighed down in your experience of darkness, of suffering?

Now imagine you have a sword in one hand and flowers in the other. What does your sword look like? Does it have jewels or shells? Don't be afraid of the sword. It is the sword of wisdom. It will not be used against anyone but rather to clear away what's attached to your dark experience, making darkness unbearable. Hold it like the Mahakali that you are, with fierceness.

What flowers do you have in the other hand? Pause. What color are they? Do they have a smell?

Notice that the words you use to describe your dark experience are growing and rising into a heap as minutes go by, as the words and images multiply. Pause and notice anything else that is hanging on to the suffering: a smell, an expression on someone's face, and so on. Lay these things down on the heap. Know that it will not grow beyond what you will allow. You have the power to hold it in place. If it runs over the edge of the carving table anyway, let it spill off the edges.

Now hold the flowers in one hand to your chest. With the other hand, cut the heap on the carving table into bits with your sword. This is not a violent cutting, but one of precision. Breathe and cut. Breathe and cut. Breathe and cut. Keep cutting so that the heap that surrounds your dark experience is in chunks.

Lay down your sword of goodwill and keep the flowers in one hand at your chest. Keep your eyes closed. Take a chunk of the heap in your hands. See into it. What is inside the heap, inside your darkness? Are there things you didn't know were there? Is it soft enough to squeeze? Is it hard? Are there tiny rocks of leftover boulders from long ago that you can use to build something with? Might there be seeds inside to plant? Have your tears provided moisture? You are not looking for what's good in darkness but for what was already in the dark experience that you could not see. We are simply seeing into darkness. Can you remain in this discovery of your dark experience in which your distorted ideas have been cut, sliced, made smaller? What is the dark experience trying to tell you? Avoid trying to find the lesson, but find a new texture, a new feeling to darkness in your life. The lesson will take you out of darkness. We are trying to remain, to be with the dark, to see its potential. What potential does your darkness have?

Lay the flowers down on the heap, on your dark experience. Give your blessing to darkness for having arrived. Give thanks to the dark mothers within you for their destruction of things needing to be destroyed.

Sit and breathe. Be in this darkness—one that is spacious and open, in chunks, but still without light. The incubation and protection of the dark experience is needed at this time in your life. It is earth, it is fodder, it is mud to help you ascend and not to see the light so much.

When you are ready, read the following ending meditation out loud, slowly, breathing between each word.

Meditation

Touch the darkness that is this life.
Live fully in devastation, knowing it as renewal and
awakening.

Carry both sword and flowers in protection of the sanctity
of all life.
I am this darkness, vast and serene.
I am the darkness that is full, open, and pure.

Please pause, breathe. Journal. Take a walk. Come back when
it is time to move forward. It could be the next hour, the next
week, or the next month. When you return, continue clockwise to the south gate. Mama Black Panther is waiting for you.

SENSING IN THE WILDERNESS OF DARKNESS

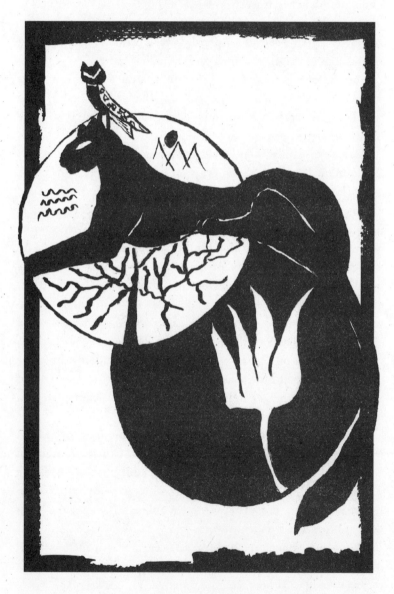

Mama Black Panther

Black Panther symbolizes courage, valor, beauty, grace, challenge, and rites of passage. Black Panther as mother is a courageous guardian, blessed with ancient maternal lunar power, who is drawn toward solitary people. Fierce feminine power resides within Black Panther. She is comfortable in her own skin, beauty, and grace. Black Panther likes to take quick, decisive action. She can assist in meeting your hidden fears and increase your awareness, especially after a period of deep suffering. She reminds us that there is medicine within our fears.

She is known as a mother of the earth who can awaken your inner passions, as well as guide and protect you. The black panther is often called the *ghost of the forest*, silently stalking and blending in with the night. She is my spirit animal or familiar.

To have a familiar who knows the forest as a panther does is to have a spirit or entity who can get you through the thick parts of life. As a black woman, I find this talent of going through the thick and tough things in life makes Mama Black Panther a likely companion in my walk with darkness. When I read something Alice Walker wrote many years ago, I felt the black panther belonged in my mandala. In Walker's novel *The Temple of My Familiar*, the animals, or familiars, in relationship with the black women reveal that such relationships are important to our awakening and freedom. Mythical and magical animals help bring forth the goddesses within the black women characters and therefore within humanity. In the same way, Mama Black Panther is present to assist us in gaining freedom within the dark experiences of life, including the minimization of motherhood and matriarchal lineages and anything that binds us culturally, politically, and spiritually.

Familiars throughout many cultures are divine messengers with the ability to hear and see on behalf of humans. Our relationships to animals in ancient times were always divine, but this was lost in the name of progress. A hierarchy of being was set in place centuries ago that made humans dominant over other animals. Before that time, it was the other way around.

We are not alone in the dark. To feel joined by a divine messenger of darkness requires feeling oneself as that first. And feeling oneself is to be awake to what life presents.

In this gateway we will walk together through the dark earth, understanding that we have been endowed with the same senses as Mama Black Panther. If we can awaken these senses and fine-tune them, perhaps our fears of darkness and blackness will lessen.

Embodying your dark self, inner and external (or both, for many of us), is to enter the mystery of our lives with all its wildness and dreams. In this gateway, we go into the dark wilderness of our lives, a wilderness we lost when we became *citified* and civil.

This is not a call to become anything other than what you already are, whether you know it or not. Instead of turning the light on in the rooms of your dark life, I offer you Mama Black Panther as a familiar, to remind you of your innate keen senses and powerful magic ability to navigate the darkest places. Black Panther represents the darkness and blackness that is not out to hurt you, even though you may be hurt in the process of seeing and awakening.

We don't know what's ahead, so we constantly live in the forest of life. Instead of avoiding what lurks behind every tree, ready to attack, consider what might be behind the trees that is waiting to support your life. What needs to reveal itself to you? Darkness dares us to stare it in the face.

My sisters and I would run out of the room at the sound of an Alfred Hitchcock movie about to appear on TV. His patented drawn-out "Good evening" and widened eyes caused our hearts to beat in double time. In seconds, we were terrorized. We couldn't change the channel quick enough. When I rediscovered Hitchcock movies as an adult, I realized that the background music, strange acting, screams, and unexpected acts of murder all worked together to create an atmosphere of suspense and anticipation. Something bad was happening. Something was coming into our lives that wasn't going to feel good. Hitchcock played on our dread—our fear of heights, betrayal, guilt, and the chaos we live with every day.

Hitchcock's movies reminded me that one of the most potent elements of darkness is its suspense. Have you ever felt as though you were simply in limbo, in the middle of nowhere in your life? Darkness as suspense can bring excitement, frustration, or fear. It brings uncertainty. Hitchcock created uncertainty in his movies to turn our attention toward the things we were afraid of. He was not interested in making us happy or peaceful; he dropped us directly in the pit of struggle. We were not surprised by the darkness in his films but were held in suspense long enough to watch the trouble unfold. Haven't you sat and watched, with great suspense and discomfort, the difficulties in your life unfolding? We try to stop it by thinking into the future, planning how to prevent the trouble and suffering before we are suffering. We abandon the trouble by distracting ourselves. We change the channel, so to speak.

Many are surprised when dark experiences show up, but many are not surprised by the darkness that repeatedly appears. We've experienced it in the past. We are aware of it in the present. And we expect it in the future. Each time darkness has been present, no matter what form or expression it takes, suspense is the initial experience. What if we use that moment of being suspended in darkness as a place in which to stop and discern what is coming before the emotions surface, before we enter the realm of terror? We know something is coming. It is in the suspense that our perceptions—of what we haven't even heard, seen, smelled, or touched—take over, and we are anxious to get out of the situation that will make us uncomfortable, whether the discomfort is real or imagined. My sisters and I were not willing to wait and see what Hitchcock had to offer. The suspense was more unbearable than the darkness headed our way. We presumed by his introduction that he was promising some kind of horror story. Later, I came to realize that Hitchcock wasn't producing horror at all.

I don't know about my sisters, but I eventually stayed still long enough to see just what was coming from Hitchcock's dark films. What I saw was a presentation on the darkness of being human. He allows us to look upon our desire to see (and even fear) how dark humanity can be. Rather than uphold a sense of darkness and blackness as repulsive, Hitchcock lets the audience sit suspended in air and watch how each character deals with individual and collective dark matters. Hitchcock lets you see everything and everyone in the shadow. His art deals completely with the absence of light.

In the state of suspense related to darkness, what sounds, tastes, smells, and sights stimulate your fear?

If you were a black panther that walked low to the ground on four legs, you would have to use your senses in the forest to sort out what you imagine and fear from what is really there in the dark. Is it there for your survival? Is it something that will harm you? In the suspended moment, you can discern within darkness. You can sense in the suspension what is before you and what's only in your mind—what is true and what is not. Do you trust yourself in the darkness? As soon as the suspense arises around a dark mood, a difficult circumstance, a dark, moody person, or a dark-skinned person, we can stop and use our honed senses to interact in darkness. We can utilize our direct sight, insight, taste, and smell, like Mama Black Panther, to see clearly whatever is before us.

Human beings are natural hunters and predators. Living in the modern world doesn't negate our ancestral lineage skilled at primal survival. Our feelings of being afraid of the dark are imprinted on our bones in part because we were vulnerable to large predators in our ancient past. How we feel, perceive, and think about darkness comes through these imprints. Likewise, our instincts for being in the dark forest were honed for hundreds of years by our ancestors (humans and other animals) and were passed to us in birth. They remain imprinted on our bones and can be accessed and used in navigating unsettling times.

Do we trust ourselves while groping in the dark? Our intense terror of darkness and blackness, beyond our innate fear of predators, is not characteristic of who we are—it is emblematic of what we have become. Over time we grow less and less afraid when our experience of darkness is unique in the moment and not what has been taught to or imposed upon us for the sake of world order.

Sensing the Dark Earth

Perhaps we can't trace how we personally lost connection to our sense of comfort with the dark earth, but we can track when we return repeatedly to that place of suspension—the pause—in the dark. Let's put our paws to the ground and track in the way we know how.

A consciousness of darkness through the senses already exists within us. We are equipped for it. Our own animal instincts, if trusted, can lead us to what is true about our situations with dark matters, dark experiences, and relationships with dark people. The senses, because of their primal nature, can reveal an authentic experience with the primordial darkness, meaning a relationship that is *not* completely influenced by what has been taught or imposed.

I am fortunate to have experienced darkness brought on by Lakota sweat lodge ceremonies. Your senses are keen when you cannot see with your eyes. At the same time, you can lose a sense of everything and everyone around you in such darkness.

I'd like to share this story. Upon entering the sweat lodge, I crawled in on all fours and traveled clockwise, feeling small rocks against my knees, smelling the cedar burning, and tasting my dried-out mouth. I felt like a four-legged relative, crawling and grunting. I dropped my hind legs and took a seat on the dirt floor. More people came in, one by one. We had all offered tobacco (something of the earth) to the one who would lead the prayers and to the one who would carry in the hot rocks for the ceremony.

The fire keeper brought in twenty-eight hot lava rocks (representing ancestors of the fire realm) one by one. That meant it was going to be an extremely hot lodge and it was going to pull the deepest prayers from us all. We sang to the ancestors and greeted them. The door of the lodge closed—nothing and no one could be seen with the eyes we came in with. The heat rose. The prayers began, and the hot ancestors spoke through the sizzling and whistling hot rocks as water was poured on them. I listened like an animal in the dark. I was unafraid of this darkness because I had been in the lodge many times before.

However, this time, I suddenly couldn't tell where the center of the lodge was. I heard someone singing and speaking prayers in the west, but I had seen that person sit on the north side before we closed ourselves in. I heard a voice on the south side, but I knew that person to be sitting in the east. Water was poured in the center over the hot ancestors, but it seemed as if the water was being poured toward the back side of the lodge. I was lost. I tried to open my eyes wider, but it was too dark to see. I became anxious, not knowing the reason I was suspended in the lodge. I started to panic, but quietly. I was glad no one could see my eyes darting back and forth for no reason—you can't use your physical eyes to see in the lodge. You can only see with your heart.

I wanted to yelp, but my heart led me to touch the earth instead. The small rocks I was seated upon felt good in my claws. I said to myself, "You're sitting on the earth." I smelled the smoke of the cedar, sage, and sweetgrass being offered over and over again. The hot rocks sizzled. The songs grew louder. The weeping of the ancestors came through us, and we almost sounded like roaring, snorting, and hissing animals in a dark forest. I used my senses to calm the fear of being lost in the dark. I could smell, touch, hear, and more. We are generally not used to letting our bodies lead us to freedom. We feel that our mind, our intellect, knows more. But in the sweat lodge, intellect doesn't work.

This is the way of being in the dark. The Inipi ceremony (as Lakota sweat lodges are called) brought me into this sense of primordial darkness that initially caused fear because of my disconnection to the earth. When I settled into the sounds and smells, there was no danger in the darkness. There was only my mind working overtime.

Life is dark as the sweat lodge. When has your mind painted a horrible picture of your dark experience in daily life? Maybe it always does this because of what you were taught about what can happen to you in dark experiences or just what can occur by being in the dark. Even though I had difficulty breathing in the lodge, when I listened to the prayer songs with the divine sense of a familiar and touched the earth, the lodge became a connection to earth, and it cleansed my mind of the notion that the darkness was a bad situation. I was less afraid of what I couldn't see.

Was there a time when you could not see in the dark (physically or mentally) and you dreamed of all kinds of horror? When you started to see again, did you realize that nothing from your mind was true?

The darkness is not as bleak a situation we might feel it is. We may cry in the lodge, but that doesn't mean it is a miserable or dreary time. It may be difficult to breathe in the heat, yet at the same time the heat of the ancestors is opening us to them as we sit in the dark, feeling into our lives. We may even feel pitiful in this unknowing dark, and at the same time we are certain we will be transported through the suffering, as we have been many times before.

Often when I leave a lodge, I avoid eye contact with the other sojourners. I don't want anyone to see my naked soul. My eyes are not actually open, anyway. It only looks like it. I am still seeing from the inside, from the dark. I have just been born from the lodge. I have been in many lodges, and each time I come out naked as to who I think I am. I drop my face and greet the others with my head down. I head toward my tent as soon as possible.

Once after a lodge, I was walking in my wet dress in the dark to my tent. I was so wobbly it would probably have been best if I had crawled, but I couldn't do so on the rough road with its cacti and snakes, none of which could be seen in the dark of the red canyon below or the mesa above. I kept walking as best I could until I realized that I had been walking for a while, and my tent was nowhere in sight. I was lost again, just as I had been in the lodge. Right then, hundreds of locusts started flying into my face. I couldn't see them in the dark; I could only feel their slimy bodies on my skin.

I started to panic, but not for long. I smelled the dirt and smoke on my sweat lodge dress. I remembered the songs and the prayers in the dark. Suddenly, I heard the laughter of the lodge chief. I turned around. I could see the fire for the lodge far in the distance, shooting up in the dark night. I headed toward the laughter and the flames. My tent was about a hundred feet ahead, tucked between two trees. The only way I knew I had arrived was the smell of a piece of sap from the juniper tree I had burned on a coal before leaving. When the tree is sick, it produces the sweetest-smelling sap, which can be used as medicine to cleanse and calm the soul.

When I reflected back on that night of being lost, I realized my panic had emerged in the temporary disconnection from the earth. The dark taught me that when I can't sense what is before me, anxiety will lead me away from my own life. If I had let my panic take over in the lodge, I would have been separated from the prayer songs to the ancestors. I would have been lost and confused. All that happened that night revealed a truth about darkness: *It is not a shadow of our lives. It is our lives.* Darkness holds all of what occurs to us. It touches us and veils our faces in the torment as we search for ourselves.

To sense darkness is to touch it. It is to get down on all fours and discover how darkness moves in your life. The fear of it dissolves once you experience that more often than not darkness is there for you. If your senses are keen, you can make a quick, decisive assessment as to whether darkness has come to hurt you or help. You can put your hands on the ground and know yourself to exist in the dark and through that survive. When you blend in with darkness, as Mama Black Panther does, you are not separate from it. You *are* it. Your life is this darkness. To fear darkness is to fear your life. This fear then becomes a hindrance to what you are here to give birth to in this world.

We know that fear holds us back, but rarely are we told that it often comes from our judgment and misunderstanding. Darkness comprises a wholeness, not just its individual events, circumstances, or incidents. All darkness—past, present, and future—is experienced as whole and simultaneously. It is one experience of the body, mind, and spirit. It is an experience of awakening and being horrified all at once.

Darkness moves. It crawls and climbs. It sits still. It dances. It moves you around the sweat lodge until you are lost, so that you don't know who is seated in the west, east, south, or north. Only you can discover how darkness sounds, smells, tastes, feels, and looks in your life.

Dancing in the Dark Wilderness

Most of us live far from wild land and wild animals and therefore from our wild ancestral ways of sensing the dark. In essence, many of us can no longer see the darkness dancing or dance ourselves in the darkness in the way of our ancient, ancient ancestors. While we have parks, land preservations, animal reservations, camping grounds, and trails to walk, it is difficult for us to access the pure wild living of our human past, so we have lost our sense of being wild and have become tame. We are civilized. We have removed ourselves from being covered in dirt, and we have perfumed the true smell of our flesh. The animals around us were tamed and made civil as well. Wild dogs, cats, goats, birds, chickens, cows, horses, and more have been made dependent upon and forced into servitude to us, just as some humans were tamed to serve other human beings for centuries. A wild human is rare to come by.

A wilderness is an area of land undisturbed by humans. What we have today are humans unshaken by the wilderness. A wilderness was a place where wild humans could live and access wild food to forage. The infrastructure the wild human relied upon for survival remained simple and aligned with what the land could give. If one is mostly living in this wilderness, they are in the elements, and in the darkness.

Is it possible to return to our wild selves? I say it is possible for us to reclaim our wild nature. Many of us make an effort by living next to wild forests, rushing rivers, and looming mountains. And yet, these places of wilderness have always been within us, and we can recognize again our wild selves and way of being when we are near such nature. Once the sound of an ocean was transmitted to us, we never forgot. You cannot forget a canyon as deep as the sky is high above. We are transfixed by images of indigenous tribes who still live in the wild because we remember ourselves in such a way. To return to the dark wilderness is to remember. Darkness helps us remember the wilderness. The appearance of darkness and dark experiences can remind us of our wild nature.

Our wild selves may feel uncomfortable in a world that has come away from the wilderness. We all have stories of when we were told to act right, to behave, to speak "properly," to do this and that so that we might fit "correctly" into society. At the same time, there was a wild animal in us trying to get out. You can use that wild animal, the familiar within, to open to the absence of light.

Mama Black Panther, your grace and courage in darkness show me how to walk in the world. Your image and energy carry me through the thick forest of life. Together, we resist that which threatens well-being, including corruption and despair. Together, we rest in the dawn, expecting the dark in which we will once again hunt only for that which keeps us alive.

GUIDED STILLNESS TWO

Being with a Familiar
Working with the Sense of Mama Black Panther Within
South Direction
Taking the Appropriate Action in Dark Experiences

Take your dharma seat in the south direction. Take a deep breath and release very slowly. Repeat this process a number of times. Breathe in your own rhythm.

Read the blessing as if someone like myself is blessing you on your journey. Read slowly, breathing between words.

Blessing

When it is time, may Mama Black Panther
walk before you, clearing the path in the dark.
May Mama Black Panther walk alongside you, teaching
you to discern truth in the darkness of your life.
May Mama Black Panther walk behind you, watching over
you and protecting you from harm.

Guided Stillness

As before, call up your particular suffering of darkness in this
moment. Pause. It can be a recent move, trouble at work, an
argument with a parent. Feel free to use the same struggle you
worked with in the first gateway.

Breathing in and breathing out, notice the animal of your
own being. Say to yourself, "This animal remembers." Breathing
in and breathing out, say, "My struggle is renewal taking place.
It is awakening taking place."

Choose a familiar—an animal you feel has magic for you
or that you feel is divinely empowered and that will walk with
you (or has in the past). Please note that you are not finding
or using your *spirit animal* as practiced in indigenous Native
American or African traditions unless you have been given that
animal spirit through ceremony or divination by medicine people of that culture.

Now that you have chosen your familiar, what does it
look like? Are there any distinguishing marks? Does it make a
sound—a growl, whistle, or bark?

Make sure your divine familiar is not leashed in any way for
this exercise. Continue to look upon it in admiration as you
face what you are suffering.

Ask the familiar, "Would you come with me into the dark
forest?" You are asking it to be with you during these dark times.
If you have a familiar from the sea, ask it to come with you
deeper into the sea.

As you take off together, notice if you are moving in unison, neither of you slower or faster than the other. Breathing in and out, you create a rhythm in darkness together.

Maybe your familiar has wings and it flies alongside you as you walk. Maybe your familiar has a tail that is wagging. Maybe your familiar is quite large—a whale, bear, or elephant. If it is a horse, don't ride it at this time. You're just moving along together.

The familiar is not here under involuntary servitude but is here teaching you how to be close to the earth—how to navigate the unknown, pain, and suffering by sensing each moment. Allow your senses to interrupt the story of pain in which emotions can block feelings. Sensing helps any paralysis. What are you smelling, hearing, seeing? Is what you sense true to the moment, or has it been distorted by past or future thinking?

What are you noticing in the dark forest? Perhaps the moon, the stars, the smell of trees. Can you feel the earth beneath you?

Move closer to your familiar. Ask, "How shall I engage this dark time in my life?" What is the familiar's message? Listen. Use your intuition. What does the familiar suggest?

Now let the familiar take the lead. Follow it and mimic its every move. Sniff, peer around trees, slow down, stop to drink water if there is a creek in your forest, look up, down, behind. You have nothing more than your senses to deal with the dark experience.

Now stand still with your familiar. Stand close. Close enough to *become* the familiar. Blend into being the familiar. Breathe in and out. You are changing shape.

Suddenly, you realize you are walking with four legs, or flying with two wings, or your legs are much like those of a sandhill crane. Maybe you can't see forward, only from side to side, as your eyes are on the sides of your face.

What is it like being the familiar? How does the forest feel after your shapeshifting? Can you feel your body sensing the forest? What senses are most awake as you engage what is in the dark forest of your life at this time? Smell, taste, touch.

You are returning to your wild self. Perhaps you are from the lineage of horses, or buffalo, or butterflies.

Suddenly, you hear a noise. You stop, look, and listen. You have no bias, no urge to determine what is good or bad. What is it? Is it for you or against you? It's very dark, so seeing with your eyes is problematic. You have only your other senses to help you determine things. Maybe what is lurking is not growling or barking. You just hear footsteps on dry leaves or twigs cracking. Breathe.

There are only a few things to do: wait, be suspended, keep sensing, and go forward.

What do you sense of your suffering at this time? Not what happened in the story of it, but what is the smell of it, the texture of it? Let go of the details of the suffering story for now.

Use your divining and intuitive skills as a familiar might before taking action.

What action did you take? Was it based in the wisdom that came from sensing, or was it a knee-jerk reaction or an action that came from fear? Pause and breathe.

Now step back into your own shape, your own body. Are there still some remnant feelings of having the body of your familiar? Breathe while holding this experience.

Turn and thank your familiar for letting you use their body to experience something different from horror, rage, anger, or helplessness in the dark experience.

Now move together toward home. It's still dark, but you now have a sense that you can be with the darkness in wellness, even if fear or terror arises.

When you are ready, read the following meditation out loud, slowly, breathing between each word.

Meditation

I rely on my wild animal self,
touching into darkness with my whole body,
returning to the wilderness of darkness over and over,
to come home, to give birth in the darkness of my life,
while singing about the earth.

Please pause, breathe, and take a break as needed. Write down your thoughts and feelings; perhaps go for a walk. When it is time to continue, come back. That time could be in the next hour, or not for another month.

Continue moving clockwise and meet Mama Dantor in the west gate.

CHILDHOOD FEAR OF DARKNESS

Mama Dantor

Mama Dantor (also called Erzulie Dantor) is the queen of the universe in Haitian culture. In other religions they call her the Black Virgin or Black Madonna. According to Mambo Rozalene, a Vodou high priestess in Haiti who I consult with from time to time (with a translator), "Mama Dantor, when on the astral plane, is called Massoula." Another name for Mama Dantor, said Mambo Rozalene, is Asofya. She also said she is called Saint Barbara in Haiti, as many Haitians are Catholic. All initiates and priestesses/priests of Haitian Vodou serve Mama Dantor. She lives underwater. She lives in the earth. Even in the cemetery you find her. She lives in darkness; she lives everywhere. I include her as a dark mother, but practitioners of Vodou would not use such terminology. Also, I am not sharing a Vodou perspective of her as much as I am using the research and conversations I had with others about this deity. Every high priest or priestess of Vodou has their own pantheon of spirits that they work with, many of which have never been heard of in the Western world, such as Massoula and Asofya.

Mama Dantor is the mother of the earth. She loves all her children and often appears with a child or children, as in the image I have included here. There is a story that says Mama Dantor's tongue was severed so that she could never tell the secrets of the medicine. The child she holds is named Anais. She has the critical role of being Mama Dantor's translator. It is a story I found interesting, though it is not a story often associated with Mama Dantor. But I decided to use it in a guided stillness exercise below.

The popular story of Mama Dantor is that she is a revered mother who protects all women and children. When I say "women," I suspect today this would include all who identify as nonbinary, gender fluid, trans, lesbian, and so forth. With her sword (pictured beneath her arm in my rendition of her) she also protects the oppressed and the abused—all the children of God.

I was told that during slavery in Haiti, the people began to use the dark and fiery side of their guiding spirits. I am using that side of Mama Dantor in this text. It was this fiery side that warriors used in ending slavery in Haiti. The French who colonized Haiti said the warriors were using "black magic," which is what they called Vodou. It is not black magic. It is a religion and a way of life. The colonizers' fear of Vodou still lives on in the many people today who perceive Vodou as dangerous, unsacred, or the devil's work. To the contrary. While many have misused this medicine, the darkness of Vodou is where you can find who you are in the same way one might find themselves through Buddhism. The French did not understand the power of a religion and perceived the darkness within it as counter to awakening. Vodou is awakening.

We will use the energy of Mama Dantor in discovering how you appear in darkness, her as mother and you as child. In this gateway, your child self is present in the darkness.

In this third gateway, we are born and our senses are fine-tuned like Mama Black Panther's. When we are born our direct experience of life is with what we hear, smell, taste, see, and touch. Here, we reflect on our childhood sense of darkness and how we carried what we perceived into our adulthood. Do you remember being ushered indoors when the sun dropped or knowing you were supposed to be indoors at night? Did you wear much black as a child? Did your parents grab your hand at the sight of a black person? Who or what was presented as scary in the movies you watched as a child? Many of us have had experiences as children that drove us to see darkness as frightening. Fear or terror was ingrained in us. For some of us, our dark experiences were catastrophic and helped create a sense that darkness is to be avoided at all costs. Early in our lives, darkness became the place where horror lived.

When I was seven, I would do whatever I could to keep from going to bed at night. When it seemed that it was inevitable, I would whine. Once in bed, I would talk my younger sister's ear off. My mother would yell, "Earthlyn, is that you talking?" It was a trick question. If I answered in the affirmative with my distinctive low voice, I would be confessing to the crime. If I said no, I would be lying, and my mother would know it. If I stayed quiet, well, it would be obvious I was just pretending to be asleep, because she had clearly heard me talking. I always chose the latter. Eventually, the silence took me over, and I fell into the state of sleep that I avoided every night. I was afraid of what would happen to me while I was asleep. Would I return from the nightly pseudodeath? My bedtime prayer included the words "If I should die before I wake . . ." In trying to stay awake, I was trying to save myself, to survive the unknown.

We avoid darkness in an attempt to save ourselves. We carry throughout life the childhood notion that the dark is out to get us. The monster is underneath our beds or in the closet. In fact, the darkness *is* in the room. For some, this darkness may have appeared in the form of sexual abuse—a tragic experience that cannot be understood by a child's mind but that shapes a child's relationship to darkness. We may have learned early in life to avoid dark people to save our life. As a child, my fear was more of what I might encounter in my sleep. Often, I would go through some kind of altering experience at night and end up falling out of the bed. I'd yell for my mother. She'd come in and tell me that I had been riding on a witch's broom because I had dry spit on the side of my mouth (which is to say I had been traveling in an unseen world). Then she'd grumble and put me back to bed.

The whole family had to be up and out the door by 5 am, because we owned one of three major childcare centers in Los Angeles during the 1960s. At dawn, I found it difficult to wake up and would fall back to sleep in the bathroom, hogging the space from my sisters. In the afternoon, I refused to take naps. It wasn't so much about going to bed; I was not keen about the darkness of my bedroom, the darkness sleep brought, and the possibility of dying while asleep. They say fear of the dark is a childhood developmental phase that comes into being around the age of two and can last far beyond. We learn that things happen in the dark. Like being thrown out of your bed and your mother talking about you riding brooms with witches. What was I doing hanging out with witches, and where were they? Who were the witches who came for me at night? What else did my mother know that she wasn't telling me?

One thing that is true, children are curious. They usually want to know about everything. Curiosity about the dark is the best place to hone our capacity to open to it. What is inside of the dark? Can it be a place of discovery, despite our fear that comes from preconceived notions? If we consider darkness as something that pries our hearts and minds open to discover more of life, then our experience of the dark may transform the *fear of a child* into the *discovery of a child*. We can look around in our troubled lives with a sense of not knowing. We can see our dark experiences, hold them as darkness encountered for the first time. We need not pretend we are unafraid of the dark because we should have gotten over such a thing by the time we reach adulthood. It doesn't matter if the hand we use to reach into the dark is trembling or steady. The question is whether we are reaching at all.

I was embarrassed of my fear of the dark as a girl. I thought of it as a weak trait—a girlish thing. And I didn't want to be distinguished from boys, with their so-called strength, because of that fear. I felt deep down I was as strong as folks said boys were. I began to practice walking into my dark bedroom without turning on the light. I wanted to prove to myself that I wasn't afraid. My mother would laugh at me upon my return from these rituals. She knew what I was doing. The fear that lingered on my face afterward gave me away each time.

My mother's laughter said she wasn't afraid, which meant she knew something about courage. Yet she was not able to guide me on the path of darkness. She didn't take my hand and talk to me about the dark.

When you were a child, did anyone ever help you withstand darkness? Did they take you by the hand and walk you over to the dark closet and tell you about the treasures inside? Did they tell you that you came from a sweet, dark place that was as dark as your bedroom at night? Did they tell you that your beauty comes from the same darkness as the night? When you were in pain, did they inform you that suffering was a bad situation rather than an eye-opening one? Most likely you were offered a night light. Perhaps a kiss on the cheek. Perhaps the dark was there for you in a way you didn't understand and in a way your parents didn't understand either.

We turn on the lights the minute the sun drops. Many of us bring our electronic devices with us to bed these days. They provide both light and entertainment while the dark awaits us. We hope that we fall asleep quickly when the lights go out. To ensure this we engage with sleeping aids, like watching TV, listening to music, calling a friend and gossiping. We find whatever means we can to help us deal with the anxiety of descending into the dark, where we will lie for hours without any control of our lives. We might wonder if we'll ever see the light of day again, but do we ever say it out loud?

What is in our minds about darkness was placed there when we were children. It is possible that our fear of darkness surfaced in the womb. It is unknown to us, and even knowing the timing of when our fear arrived does not resolve it. Our fear is generational and ancestral. It is old and deep in the pores of our flesh. This is the reason it is important to reflect on our childhood experiences in meeting our fear of darkness. In childhood, we were still close to the essential darkness we emerged from into life. In mining our childhood, we can discover the impact of being severed from the darkness of our mother's womb and how it might have led to disconnecting from the dark earth for a lifetime.

Reflecting on Childhood Experiences of Darkness

As children we generally feel that we have no control over our lives. It's bewildering to be a child without control who has to experience darkness. We feel unprotected. Our childhood fears of darkness may relate to our developing awareness that the world is not as it appears. As we begin to see and know more about the world, that can cause confusion and feelings of unsafety. This confusion is part of the unfolding of the child self in the dark.

It was through a process of awareness in the dark that I discovered being black was unacceptable. Everything seemed distorted, and I was unable to understand my place in a world skewed toward whiteness. As I grew, my experience of life in a dark body was constantly being uncovered. Was I going to have a life filled with loss? My changing reality made nightmares seem real.

Can you think back on your own childhood and sense a time when you did not feel a part of the world? Suddenly, you realized you were different, and the fear of that difference brought terror, because you didn't know what would become of you in the vast darkness of uncertainty. Being different is often deemed a dark experience.

What if the lack of control in the darkness, as in sleep, could be the beginning of opening to darkness? What if my feeling unacceptable as a black child was the beginning of seeing black skin through an unencumbered and unpoliticized darkness? Of course, we can only develop such understandings of our experiences as adults, but later in life is better than never.

As a child, sleep was my portal to opening to the dark. I was too young to see it that way. I had a number of recurring childhood dreams that would bring up real feelings of being sucked into darkness. I dreamed of a red fox that chased my mother and me. I was six years old. The fox hid and then ran after me and my mother, standing upright on his two hind legs. He was faster than a dog, so we had to run hard to get away. We were chased down busy Arlington Avenue, where we lived in Los Angeles. No one saw us. There were no cars on the usually busy street. There was no one to save us. We crossed Washington Boulevard and continued to run until we reached the library across from the convent where nuns and "wayward" girls were sequestered. I thought of the girls and wanted to be sequestered like them, but I was neither Catholic nor wayward. The red fox continued to chase us, but stopped when we entered through the library's doors made of beveled glass and heavy oak. When the doors shut behind us, I woke up, breathing hard and alone in my bed, in the dark. My younger sister was sound asleep in her bed next to mine. I wanted to wake her, but I didn't.

The dream stimulated the sense of not having control and also that of being unprotected. Even my mother could not stop the fox. In the darkness, there is often no one to save us from what we are afraid of. We discover this early in life—that we have no control over things that happen in the dark experiences of our lives. We may have questioned whether our parents or guardians provided enough protection in the world. We learned that they were human and vulnerable, too. My parents knew they couldn't really save their black daughters from hatred, so they gave us God. I found myself relying on God and becoming increasingly religious at a very young age in order to navigate the storms of life. God was my light. Singing hymns and writing poetry were my ways of settling myself in a frightening world.

I kept expecting the fox dream to show up, and it did. I continued to see the fox at night in my sleep and remained frightened of it. The dream repeated itself for four years. When I reflected on the dream later, I saw the fox as my fear of being unprotected and having no control over my life. Plus I had to contend with being black and having no control over the dark experiences of discrimination.

I walked in the world protected only by my belief in God. My internalization of fear and hatred of darkness and blackness caused a deep rift between the world and me at a very young age. Darkness was my whole life. I was too young to know that to accept the fox in my dream was to accept my relationship with darkness, to accept a blackness that was of the rich earth. I would discover this later, well into my adulthood, through my Buddhist practice. No matter what your race or ethnicity, there can be a deep rift between you and the world when you look upon what is dark in your life with despair and distress. When you view the fox in your life, the darkness, as a portal of learning, then there is less despair and distress.

While writing this section, I had a conversation with an artist friend of mine who is a medicine woman of African descent, as well as a lucid dreamer. She shared with me this story:

As a gentle child growing up in the hood and profoundly unprotected, I developed recurring nightmares in which I was being chased by an unrelenting and hostile force. I'd run, hide, change my route, and run some more. Terrified and alone, I was on the empty streets of unknown neighborhoods, but the homes were filled with people living comfortably. Sometimes the neighborhoods would be residential, and sometimes they'd be completely abandoned industrial areas—abandoned with the exception of me: alone, terrified, running, and trying to hide. It was exhausting, and it went on for years.

One day I was so exhausted and done, I instructed myself that when I'd realize I was again in some version of that same dream, I could say no, end it, and wake up. I now believe the key was that I was motivated, and I believed that I could notice I was in a dream, and I believed I could stop it. And I still don't understand why I believed that as a child.

I'd like to say that my friend and I turned toward the darkness, stared it down. In those instances of seeing the dark forces, it was clear that the dark was not going away. In our adulthood, in facing darkness, we can end our running from it. Whether we understood anything about liberation or empowerment as children doesn't matter. It is not always necessary to understand immediately what is in front of us. But it is important to discern whether or not to go forward and continue to wrestle with the unknown.

By the time I reached adolescence, I could see what darkness gave me. I could see, in hindsight, that the fox could have been protection for my mother and me as we headed down the urban streets of Los Angeles. In real life, a fox hides so that it is not detected by any predators or so that it is not eliminated by those who want to feed on it or see it as a problem. Perhaps the fox was not chasing us but running with us in the darkness of life, trying to survive in the same way that we were.

Surviving Childhood Experiences of Darkness

A childhood fear or disdain of the dark can cause an early withdrawal from a dark world. Feelings of being unprotected increase under the weight of horrific events that happen in life. A mysterious life can be especially frightening to a child who perceives danger. When they hear stories in the news or hear their parents talking about children being taken from their families, or youth being haphazardly killed, or children being kidnapped or caught in sex trafficking, a child can't help but feel unsafe in the darkness that surrounds them. They look for safety and goodness as it is presented in movies, TV programs, churches, temples, or any other place that is deemed light. How can we assist children in understanding darkness and offer spiritual protection to them when light is not accessible?

Developmentally, children spend a great amount of time in the dark, which they experienced as not knowing, not understanding, and not having control of their lives. Most anyone can remember at some point in childhood feeling emotionally stuck—unable to continue life in such circumstances. This is what childhood is about. Children and youth are only beginning to learn about the world they are born into. This learning is filled with danger and fear. No matter where you live in the world, there will be this kind of darkness for our children and youth. How can we as adults assist the young in understanding the *sacred portal* through which they will encounter the rest of their lives?

I suspect the rise of bullying in this country indicates that the young do not know how to handle or control the crises in their families and in the world. Bullying is not necessarily the result of a personality imbalance. Disciplining the bully and comforting the bullied don't always help facilitate the passage through the childhood developmental phase of darkness. Even a child who appears joyful may simply be presenting as happy as a coping skill to deal with the unknown aspects of growing emotionally and physically in vast darkness. If the childhood phase of darkness, which lasts at least eighteen years, is ignored or seen solely in terms of psychological and social development, a crisis of the heart and mind will fester in children, leading to further destructive action—and not the kind that fosters ascended humanity.

They will become the kinds of warriors who battle their own inner territory without regard to those around them. Some will gravitate toward substance abuse, sexual abuse, consumerism, or forms of violence. They will go deeper into the abyss without understanding the role of darkness in their lives as sacred time.

Inside my childhood experiences with darkness was the fear of not knowing how I would survive. It created an obsession with knowledge, with wanting to know what was next, wanting to know how to live a life in which darkness seemed to consume and maybe even chase me. With that obsession, I got baptized in the Church of Christ when I was eleven. I went on to earn the highest educational degrees possible. I participated in social justice movements. I explored the worlds of African, Native American, and Buddhist rituals and ceremonies.

As frightened children, we find ways to slay the monsters. The problem comes when we can no longer fight and are unable to stay with the darkness. We are taught to wait for the light. But as children, we have not yet developed the virtue of patience. Perhaps for that reason we see a marked increase in suicide among tweens and teens, as the light promised them is not realized fast enough for children who now live in the world of instant everything. They lose faith and trust in adults who have offered solutions that don't seem to eliminate the darkness that cannot be eliminated.

Assisting Young People Through the Portal of Darkness

I remember the moment when, at the age of fifteen, I realized that trouble in life was here to stay. After it happened, I became silent. Every day seemed to drone on. I observed everyone swirling about as if they had no problems at all. I wondered what they were doing with their suffering. Had they accepted some kind of fate or destiny in the cracked promise of salvation? Even those I knew who relied on God seemed to suffer as much as those who didn't.

It happened one day after class in high school. The loud, blaring bells that ring at the end of the day covered the sound of the gunshot.

A friend of mine, who was raised a devout Catholic, had killed herself. A little before her suicide, my friend had shared with me that her mother did not like her. I offered to let her stay with me and my family after she told me the details, but only two days later her body was found behind the gas station across from the school. I had been waiting for her at the bus stop. Someone who knew we were friends ran to tell me what had happened. I tried to go find my friend, but folks held me back. "Don't go over there," they said.

Later, I felt as though the whole world had failed her. No one knew how to deal with the dark experiences we young people were suffering. We were all left to fend for ourselves without being ushered and watched over by those older than ourselves. We were without the necessary skills to live with a dark, challenging, but sacred world. How can our youth be empowered in the realm of darkness and be aware of the nature of life as it is?

Awareness from within dark experiences comes in its own time. But this does not mean that we can't teach one another, especially young people, how to dwell in darkness. If we said to our children regarding their dark experiences, "You are in a deep, sacred time of your life. You are learning how to live," perhaps then we could teach them how to take care of themselves in this deep initiation of life. Perhaps the mindfulness being taught to youth these days could include reflection on their circumstances and what those circumstances are teaching them—not only quieting them or changing their behavior with mindfulness, but pointing youth to the vast and beautiful nature of the dark in their lives. What a powerful time for them. If we could hold troubled children, tweens, and teens as if in ceremony, we might be able to show them the benefit of the sacred portal we all have gone through. But the ones with the guiding hands must understand the riches of being in the womb, in the darkness. They must be willing to and know how to dwell in darkness and not pretend that they are not drinking and drugging or doing some of the same activities as the youth in dark times.

Young people are in the deepest dive of their lives. Can we breathe with and into them, help them to rejuvenate and prepare for the next and the next and the next experience of darkness? Instead of shoring them up only with affirmations, we can teach them how to survive until they reach the other side of their dark experiences. While we focus on academic excellence, perhaps we could balance it with acknowledging and recognizing the achievement of having survived horrific experiences. We can help youth during troubled times to receive (not necessarily accept) the darknesses of their lives as instances of nature training them to survive, so that they can reach adulthood in wellness and have the skills to continue swimming in the dark waters. We can teach that darkness has come to assist them. Patience must be learned by the young.

I am grateful my parents offered the rituals of church to me and my sisters to build upon. While Christianity spoke to me in some ways and not in others, I felt a strong enough sense of it for it to serve as a path that helped me through my teen years. I integrated the songs and prayers of Christianity with dance, poetry, art, music, and Pan-Africanism. By the time I was eighteen, I added African rituals and ceremonies to my path, and then Buddhism when I was thirty. It was important to have a road to walk while experiencing some of my deepest emotions.

I am grateful for the many communities in the world that provide rite-of-passage ceremonies for their teen populations. Community teen programs also have proven beneficial. In each of these ways, the common factor is a sense of *protection provided by adults* and a hand for them to hold as their lives unfold. The child was once a newborn fresh from darkness; that darkness intensifies in adolescence as they rebirth themselves into who they feel themselves to be. Teens need as much attention as newborns, if not more.

Children enter a world filled with strange things. I often wonder if at birth we are afraid of the light and later we transfer that fear to darkness. In both cases, there is an inability to discern what is before our eyes. This lack of sight or understanding in our youth can lead us into an unending and misunderstood odyssey through darkness.

If you see a mother who has scars on her face on this never-ending path of darkness, that is Mama Dantor. She is a warrior who knows struggle, and when a child cries out, Mama Dantor responds much like the Great Mother Prajnaparamita in the Buddhist canon. Mama Dantor will also destroy whatever needs to be eliminated to help ease or eliminate the child's cry.

Mama Dantor reminds me of my mother, who I experienced as harsh, and yet she would look upon me with love as if I were the most precious being she had ever laid eyes on. She was a black woman born in 1910 on the south bank of the Red River in Alexandria, Louisiana, where the largest amount of slave trading occurred in the United States. She was Mama Dantor who struggled to live in a world in which she was not seen and was therefore mistreated. My mother tried to protect me and my sisters from the suffering she had endured. I suspect she saw great strength in us that matched her own and thought it would make trouble for us in a world that was dangerous for strong young black girls. Even though her harshness didn't feel to me to be the best method, she may have been training me to withstand the darkness that life is, painful or not. Many mothers are Mama Dantor—fiercely protecting their children, carrying love and disdain, wielding a sword and yet having a lap soft enough for children to lay their heads upon.

Fortunately, children are talented. They can see intuitively quite well in the darkness of their lives. They are more able than adults to come into harmony with darkness, because they haven't been long out of the womb. To enhance this fresh-out-of-the-darkness quality children have is to acknowledge it and hone it for the sake of their living well. We say, "Out of the mouth of babes" when children provide clarity for us.

There is an archetype in my Black Angel oracle deck called the Moon Child. She is in the dark, and yet she can see through a star and a sliver of moon over her third eye. She speaks bluntly, without apology, because she is sure of what she sees in the dark. She is a truthsayer. She is radically honest and forthright, so much so that she might be experienced as rude. Moon Child wakes us up in the darkness with her truth. To her, the darkness is not for sleeping. It's for playing and seeing the stars. She is keenly aware of the wounding of childhood and thus remains in the dark for the healing, or for the authentic social activism she aspires to. Moon Child understands that a legacy of suffering comes with birth. Like all the dark mothers, she brings a sharp edge to cut through the dangers, to protect herself and other children from further wounding. Ultimately, Moon Child is a young Mama Dantor in training.

While parents are portals for children, our children are our portals by which we will come to love darkness as we love them, regardless of the difficulties. Our fear is old. It will take time to greet darkness as a friend, no matter how afraid or unafraid we are. Life is earth-shattering.

GUIDED STILLNESS THREE

Sweetening the Tongue
Working with the Tongue That Was Removed from
Mama Dantor, the Tongue That Holds the Medicine
West Direction
Sweetness When Speaking Within Dark Experiences

Take your dharma seat in a quiet space in the west direction. Breathe deeply and release slowly. Very slowly. Repeat this several times. After a while, breathe naturally, in your own rhythm.

Read the blessing as if someone like myself is blessing you on your journey. Read slowly, breathing between the words.

Blessing

May your child self,
having been birthed from darkness,
be protected by the sword of Mama Dantor, a loving
and fierce mother.
As you sit on her lap in the dark listening to her messages,
you become the messenger of Mama Dantor's darkness.
May you find yourself in the lap of the dark earth.

Guided Stillness

As before, consider what you are suffering in this moment. It can be the same difficulty that you used in the previous gateways. Pause.

Say this to yourself: "Breathing in and breathing out, I am aware of my body. Breathing in and breathing out, I know renewal and awakening are taking place."

Choose the main person in your story who you feel is causing you to suffer; make it someone over sixteen years old. "Breathing in and breathing out." Now shrink that person down to a child and seat that child on your lap. It is only for a short time. Breathe. Notice how you feel with the child person who you feel is causing you to suffer.

What is the child wearing? What kind of shoes? What are they doing? Smiling? Are they angry? What do you feel when you see the person (the one who seems to be causing your suffering) as a child sitting in your lap?

Allow the child person to sit with you. Try to be Mama Dantor to the child. Think of protecting the child even though they are not yours.

What is the child's name? Call them by that name, but add "little" to it. For example, *little Sean, little Aliya, little Anna* . . .

Tell little whoever, "I know that you are suffering." Pause and look into their eyes. Next, say, "I know it hasn't been easy living in this world."

Now what is the child doing? Has their facial expression changed? What are their eyes doing? Are they fidgeting, looking up, or looking down?

Pause, breathe, and look at the child. Ask the child to whisper in your ear what they are suffering. When the child whispers, what do they say? Are they telling you about their life? This is a moment in which intuition can help you discern the voice of the child. What might they have suffered in this world? Don't ask, just listen and hear what you hear. No need to have it confirmed.

Are they revealing to you what they suffer? If not, repeat, "I know that you are suffering."

If they do let you know, say, "Thank you for sharing that with me. Now I know what you suffer."

Say to the child, "I'm suffering too." Pause and breathe for some time. Then say, "And still, I promise to protect you, to not harm you."

What is the child doing now? Listening? Crying? Remaining silent? Embrace the child.

Now bring the child back to adulthood, that person who you feel caused you to suffer. Bow to them, shake hands with them, or put your hand on your heart to acknowledge doing this practice together.

We are usually quick to say to each other, as adults, things that cause further harm in dark situations. We may lash out, or we may withdraw while suppressing our feelings. Here, we are experiencing what it might feel like to sweeten the tongue amid our angst, fear, and distress. Hopefully, when you see the actual person, alongside the suffering or destruction that might have occurred, the dark experience between you will feel transformative. You can do this exercise before talking with anyone while sensitivities are high and emotions are obscuring the situation.

When you are ready, read the following ending meditation out loud, slowly, breathing between each word.

Meditation

I call forth curiosity
while surrendering to darkness,
leaving behind the control I wished for in my childhood.
I recognize my young self as having trained in darkness
throughout childhood,
and I bring that training forth in living my life today.
I can now let go of darkness as a monster in the closet,
so that I can feel the new experiences of darkness
as awakening.

Pause again. Take the time to breathe the breath you were unable to take in as a child. Write about this awakening, not as an experience, but as what you are seeing right now about the mothering of the earth, the greater mothers of the spirit world who were always with you. Take a walk. Come back when it is time to move forward. It could be the next hour, the next week, or the next month.

When you return, continue clockwise to the north gate. Mami Wata is waiting for you.

DWELLING IN DARKNESS

Mami Wata

Mami Wata is Mother of the Waters, a dark mother from Benin (formerly Dahomey). She is half human and half water being. Some may call her a mermaid. However, mermaids mean different things to different cultures. In Greek mythology, for example, mermaids were often known as sirens—half woman and half bird. Mami Wata is not a mermaid in the Greek sense, nor is she considered such in ancient African cosmology. Mermaids tend to be relegated to folklore, and Mami Wata is a water spirit who has at least a four-thousand-year-old (or longer) lineage of devotees, rituals, and ceremonies in Haiti, Benin, other parts of Africa, and other places in the African diaspora. She shares the stage with the African Caribbean and African Brazilian water deities Oshun, Yemayá, and La Sirena and the water spirits called nagas of the ancient Hindu, Buddhist, and Jain traditions. Suijin is a Shinto god of water in Japanese mythology. We could go on and on with relatives to Mami Wata.

Mami Wata is from the deepest part of the sea, where the waters are black and are considered the waters of healing. She represents our great-great-great-grandparents. She is all genders. Mami Wata is fluid, travels many places, and takes on the forms necessary to protect and provide good fortune.

With her python as the whisperer, we can follow Mami Wata's path of listening to darkness. Listen for the sustenance needed to feed us along the way, represented by the fish in her hand, which I placed there. The fish is not dead. Mami Wata is not feeding us its dead flesh as much as she is providing the capacity of water to be the deep energy or current to withstand and survive darkness over a lifetime. In my view, the flexible bones of the fish, like our bones, carry memories of the deep waters and a darkness that moves and is filled with tranquility.

In this fourth gate we slip back into the dark, watery abyss of our mother's womb with Mami Wata. We go back to the darkness from where we came. We all have experienced deep waters in swimming through life's chaos. In essence, at this gate we are being reminded that we lived in dark waters months before our appearance on earth.

In the first three gateways we began to open and accept darkness into our lives. We stood with the fierceness of Mahakali, gathering the skulls of things destroyed for the growth of humanity. We heightened the senses through Mama Black Panther and allowed ourselves to be held in the embrace of Mama Dantor. By now, in this gateway, we have considered transforming in the midst of all the destruction around us. Hopefully, we have gained an understanding of the nature of darkness as fierce and kind.

In this fourth gateway, there is still a gestation of darkness. We are still introducing ourselves to the ancestors. Maybe we feel an anxiousness to get to the light after the first three gates. We want no more talk of darkness. We may have felt unprepared for what might be in front of us if we stayed too long in a dark place. Perhaps this experience is an old one, an emotional one.

From the beginning of humanity, darkness has been tangled with our emotions—how we feel about the dark. The difficult emotions then led us away from developing a relationship with darkness and making inquiries about it. All we knew was that it didn't feel good.

The darkness we experience throughout time—felt as difficult, unbearable, or shadowy—is like the watery abyss in which Mami Wata lives. Darkness provides a sacred environment by which we can *hone intuition, insight, and wisdom* and receive what is needed. Darkness is an open awareness, despite our fear of it. When we learn how to dwell in the deep waters of Mami Wata, we are less anxious because we can imagine dark water as an environment in which to let go, suspend our stories, and breathe deeply in and out. In other words, we are brought back to our bodies and not caught in mind games centered on light.

Even when addiction, thoughts of suicide, and other difficulties are at work in our minds, our bodies will lead us, if we let them, to stillness and silence. This is not a harmful silence or censoring. It is a liberating silence, a lifestyle of darkness in which breathing through the difficult creates spontaneous meditation. We begin to see and feel in the silence what is needed to be seen and acted upon. In the deep water of Mami Wata, we allow meditation to come through rather than imposing meditation upon ourselves. Also, we are not acting upon what we *think* we should do or say to rid ourselves of darkness. Instead, we are being shown what it is we need to see in the dark before taking action. We learned some of this in the second gateway with Mama Black Panther.

Are you constantly looking for the light while in the dark? Where are you in the dark—at the surface bobbing up and down in the water, looking for a way out? Or are you suspended deep in the darkness, breathing?

The lack of perceived physical illumination in darkness has led to an interpretation of darkness as negative. But negative and positive are concepts from the realm of science. There is a need for both negative and positive poles for a battery to work. Darkness has no polarity, even though it has been assigned the pole of negative by many. Light has no polarity, even though it has been assigned the pole of positive. We can only qualitatively say that blackness is negative in the sense that it appears to be without color and is filled with suffering, although blackness is positively full of color—it contains all colors.

When we consider the greater darkness from which everyone was born and from which everything arises, we can see how we have lost sight of our dark origins and have lived inside a distorted sense of blackness and whiteness, darkness and lightness. When we speak of whiteness as supreme and blackness as inferior, we are speaking from a distortion that was created to control humanity. As a result, much of what we are tackling as human beings doesn't include an exploration and integration of darkness as itself. It is always positioned in opposition to and compared against lightness. The fight between lightness and darkness, blackness and whiteness, leads to an ancient battle for human dignity on all fronts.

We have spent centuries contemplating how to emerge from darkness from every angle—psychology, sociology, religion, politics, and so on. We have not spent time learning how to dwell in darkness. So when things become unbearable, we are more likely to withdraw from engaging life or to neglect life. We may even consider suicide when the rainbow is not enough. How do we dwell *with* darkness long enough to not kill ourselves and each other within it? Can we stay with darkness and let it show us its gold without mining for it?

I want to emphasize that dwelling in darkness in this text does not mean wallowing in sadness or pain, but being with darkness as a friend, a companion in discovering life and what we need to know of being human on a spiritual walk. Also, we don't dwell in darkness to get something out of it; we stay with it until it gets out of us what is needed to be well. We wait for the medicine.

Fortunately, darkness is always present, so this text is inviting you to be with the present, this moment. The present moment doesn't always feel good. The present moment isn't always filled with so-called light. Mostly our lives don't feel good. But we don't know what to do about it. The suggestion here is to sit with the darkness and, if necessary, seek a mental health professional who might guide you in understanding this spiritual and emotional walk with darkness as opposed to fixing it. This works only if you are ready. Hopefully, you are ready to open to life, which is to open to the absence of light in wellness and well-being.

To surpass the distortions placed upon darkness of my skin and my life, I dwelled in it. When COVID-19 first charged through the world in 2020, killing many and rendering others with an experience of the loss of freedom, I had already been sitting inside my cave, beneath the waters. I brought darkness close to my heart to listen. It required that I sit with darkness—the hard times—despite the fear of it, without knowing whether I would emerge in wellness or even alive, as life is dark, meaning that it is unknown. I spent time with my emotions and feelings. I didn't experience depression, but the devastation of the pandemic reminded me of the times I would feel as though I were drowning and there were no lifeguards on watch.

I felt prepared for dwelling in the darkness of the times. Through years of deep contemplation, meditation, rituals, and ceremonies, I was accustomed to being afraid of the expansiveness of darkness and dark experiences that drew quiet tears and even more than a few instances of what folks call "the ugly cry." Yet I stayed with the uncomfortable experience of the unilluminated and painful places in my life. I'd reach out for help at times, but still there was no eliminating this constant darkness that resided with me and everyone else I knew. I remained, and I began a practice of asking, "What is this darkness?" I asked without looking for an answer. I still ask, even though I am the author of this book.

Where there is no knowing, I remain humble and compassionate in the unknowing. This is dwelling in darkness. One can meditate for a lifetime and not be prepared for the discovery. Preparation is not possible for most of our dark experiences. What is possible is developing an increased capacity for dwelling in darkness each time we are eaten up by it. How do we survive our own disappearance?

Developing the Capacity to Dwell in Darkness

In my younger days, some called me the depressive type—a person who didn't want to be here on the planet. The term *shut down* was used to describe me once. In a psychological sense, perhaps I was that way at various times, but I didn't readily accept the diagnosis. I took it into my cave and laid it alongside me. It served as an object of concentration while sitting in the dark. I would ask the depression, "What are you?" I didn't ask, "Why are you here?" I wanted to know this thing that visited millions in the world and was often blamed in encouraging them to take their lives. Many families carry the warrior marks of depression, including my own family. Why did I choose to dwell there in the middle of depression? Because I wanted to live. Living meant dwelling in the present darkness. Even if I wasn't sure I would survive.

Each time I experienced the depth of my sadness, I saw parts of myself dying away, just as I saw the connection between my perception of the suffering and some representation of darkness. I was not going to surpass the darkness, and I was not supposed to outlive darkness like some superbeing. I was to pass through it, shedding fear like mangy fur. I would tell myself that I was going to die, and I would feel hopeless. And I did die. The "me" I thought of as myself dissolved in the blackness of things. The destruction of that "me" enabled the divine presence to live—the presence that knows love and doesn't fight against it.

The act of dwelling in the darkness of depression felt the same as dwelling in systemic oppression, which I also had no control of. I became acquainted with racism at the age of eight. By sixteen I was a veteran in the battle between whiteness and blackness, darkness and lightness. I didn't trust the folks who said darkness was abundant and radiant. I wondered how they could claim such a thing. From what place in life did they sit in their dark caves and know this to be true? Had they been on the roller coaster of depression and discovered from experience that darkness was radiant and abundant? Or had they decided something beneficial about darkness from their minds or from what they read in books? Did they ever feel that they could leave darkness behind? Had they died in the darkness, recovered, and returned from death to tell us about it?

When I began to write from my dwelling with it, darkness took its rightful place. It wasn't a bad thing, because that would mean my entire life as a dark-bodied person living in the darkness of oppression would be a bad life. I would have to get rid of such a life, wouldn't I? But the darkness that dwelled with me and in me was so expansive, there were no words for it, no psychological diagnosis. I could not write about it or call it abundant and radiant. I felt I had the capacity to stay with darkness and remain alive. Depression became a spiritual experience of being deeply sensitive and empathic. Darkness became a sacred portal for riding the waves and being thrown against the shore whole and broken.

This is not to say that I didn't need help. I always knew I needed help in mental health ways as well as in spiritual ways. But the helper would have to understand more than modalities and pharmaceutical solutions; they would have to know that mental health (which is really spiritual health) was wellness within darkness and not simply a superficial journey to the light not yet born in me.

In the past, I wrote of oppression and depression but not of the darkness they were born from. I wrote from the seeds of negativity that were placed on darkness and not of the darkness empty of the ideas placed upon it. I needed water for new seeds. I needed to dwell as Mami Wata. I needed water poured onto the fire of my words.

How is it that you dwell in darkness? If you don't, what would help you sit in darkness as a dwelling place? Perhaps you can begin settling your body by breathing and writing down what your dark places look like. Are they filled with something you have not seen before? Although doing so is an honorable act, we are not necessarily looking for wisdom in the dark. We allow the darkness to speak to us, through what we are seeing and experiencing. What are you saying to yourself about darkness? Do you feel that to be true or authentic? Where did you get your words about darkness? Where did you learn to speak of darkness in such a way? At some point, I suggest writing a letter to darkness and express what you have experienced with it. Then, you could have darkness respond in a letter back to you. See what you might discover.

I have reached into darkness without knowing it. Like the sea, darkness could not be grabbed and twisted into something for my own use. Although darkness felt like the systemic oppression I experienced, it was beyond that. All things in my life were born of this darkness—even the freedom that arises from my dark existence.

The spiritual path of darkness is for those who are willing to work with the incomprehensible: soul, spirit, and consciousness. I know this because I continued dwelling with the purity of darkness, without my ideas, until I fell in love with it. Yes, I fell in love with the wretched dark water that never reveals all of who or what it is. When you fall in love with something like darkness, you are willing to withstand the challenges of the relationship—unable to prevent what might be harmful and destructive and at the same time allowing utter destruction to awaken you. Are you willing to be killed by the divine, so to speak?

You may ask, What is there to do to prepare for dwelling in something you cannot understand, touch, or know? There is no preparing. You are taken below with Mami Wata. You wade; you suspend beliefs and personal realities for a moment. You dwell in the dark water until the longing for the sun to hover above the surface dissipates. You are where you are. Circumstances may be analyzed and critiqued, but the darkness remains, if not expanding even more.

We do not know what this darkness is, and yet we realize that it is always between us and what we are reaching for in life. Eventually, we stop and hang in the abyss. When something like a disaster, tragedy, major change in life, or political upheaval occurs, darkness is forcing us to stop and greet the unknown quality of life. In our stopping, contemplation and meditation arise on their own, without instructions or posture. You may continue reaching out in the darkness for something, but it is this wanting something that strips your ocean of its waves.

In the dark, you are no longer all-knowing. You are undone. To be undone is what sets you in place for opening to darkness.

What has thrown you in the deep abyss? Can you dwell long enough to awaken to something new about life?

As I wrote in my book *The Deepest Peace*:

> We are to be undone. This is life. There's no getting around it. We unravel over and over again. Life gets disrupted. We are thrown off. We face the unimaginable. It's sobering, ending up in a place that we thought we'd never be. In that

strange place we are quietly undone. We're not who we thought we were. We burn away, and then immediately we want to sweep up the ashes, or whittle and sand the charred pieces, to make a smooth mound of life—a mound that if breathed upon would come undone again. We create mountains from the shadows left behind by disruption, only to find out after climbing such mountains we could have just walked through them. We struggle when the waters of our lives are disturbed, and our reflections appear distorted and unfamiliar. We run from the waters. Being undone, we discover we've been fooled by wishing wells and have mistaken the fire of desire for radiance. We're stunned.

To be undone is a mystical occurrence, a state of being in which we are rendered, eyes opened, to the unknown. We see, hear, smell, taste, think, and can do nothing about it. All doing is done. What are we to do when we feel lost, a stranger in our own lives? We go through it. In the undoing of life, silence stretches into eternity—revealing stars in the dark.[5]

Are you willing to be a stranger in your own life for the sake of easing the suffering of what you think yourself to be? Do you have in place a practice of stillness and breathing? It doesn't have to be any official practice of meditation or religious method. Where and when are you still enough for the darkness to exist in all of its glory? Do you ever really sit down without distraction, even for a moment?

When I would return from those deep dives of dark experiences, I would have a handful of different ways to live my life. These ways didn't come from my mind. They were not strategies. I could tell this because I was quite frightened of the new ways of living that were given. How could I speak more truthfully from love, not anger? How could I stop hiding?

In the dark, I realize all of life is unknown, dark, and mysterious. So when I sense darkness, I know in the moment that all is well, even with pain and suffering. I can stay in suffering long enough to be born again through the waters.

If we acknowledge the origin of our birth, the dark, watery womb, and the darkness before entering the womb, then we are willing to receive everything that comes in the dark. We feel no longer stuck in darkness but nurtured by it.

A fuller vision of darkness reveals itself if we are willing to open our eyes even while our minds struggle with fear and avoidance of dark experiences, things, and people. With our eyes and palms open in darkness, we will come to appreciate its existence.

While we have and will experience pandemics, hatred, grief, and so on, we are becoming clear and developing the capacity to see the dark unknown as a place where our deepest transformation of these things occurs. In the darkness of our life, we are giving birth to ourselves constantly. Each time we recognize darkness as a vast container that holds life, it stimulates visions and creativity. The journey in the dark soon synchronizes with the life we imagine for ourselves and the world.

Once you are willing to be with life as dark—as unknown, as full of possibilities—then darkness will reveal its content and bring your awareness to what's needed to be seen and heard. You may find that you are willing to claim your seat in the watery cave dwelling of humankind.

Opening to Transformation Through Darkness

To open to Mami Wata is to open to transformation, divination, spiritual wealth, and fortune—all within destruction. Transformation requires destruction. We are constantly looking to transform so that the suffering in our lives is eased or eliminated. We may find ourselves suspended in darkness without knowing what to do about the situation other than looking for the exit. We begin to long for a lighter side of life. While we are longing for a different life in the darkness, the darkness longs for us. It pulls us further down into it the more we try to avoid it.

When we long for ourselves, we may not be aware that we are longing for the darkness in which to search for and ponder life. When we are seeking transformation, we may not know that we also are asking to be in darkness. In seeking transformation, we are using the darkness of suffering. We want to know how to live in the best way. In seeking transformation, we are asking to change our lives by descending further into darkness to discover who we are and more about this life.

Dwelling in darkness is a sacred, intentional, and compassionate act for one's own life. Often, we are dragged by our feet, kicking and screaming, down into the deep, whether we meant to go there or not. You may suffer when you discover there is no way out. You hope that someone misses you or hears your cries and checks in with you. You don't know what will become of asking for change, which is a request to know yourself more closely. The darkness welcomes your return. It has been waiting for you to discover it and to discover yourself in relationship to it.

In the early 1980s, I moved to San Francisco from my birthplace of Los Angeles. I had been hanging out with a neighbor in her downstairs apartment eating strawberries and a shrimp salad. Suddenly, my eyes began to itch. The itching was so intense I decided to leave and go upstairs to my own apartment. As I was walking up, I felt my limbs weaken and my breath grow short. By the time I entered my apartment, my breathing was labored. I ran to my window and opened it, trying to get air. But all the air passages were blocked in my body. No air could get into my lungs. My eyes began to swell and shut, and I wobbled to the bathroom. My eyes had grown to the size of golf balls. Gratefully, I could see through tiny slits if I held my head back. My whole face had swollen, and the crevices of my face were a dark purple.

I struggled to the phone and dialed 911, but I couldn't talk. My throat had closed along with my eyes. I made it back downstairs to my neighbor's apartment, nearly falling at every step. I knocked on her door. When she opened it, she gave a look that told me I was dying. She pulled me in and laid me on the bed. She stuffed an anti-histamine down my throat with her finger and said, "You're having an allergy reaction. This should help." I still couldn't breathe despite the pill. I had never experienced such a condition. I lay there in the dark, wide awake, trying to survive the unknown, which could have very well been my death. I couldn't share my fear because I couldn't talk. I was no longer functioning in my body. We had no idea how far along I was in what I came to know as my first anaphylactic shock episode.

Lying in the dark, I remained with the fear that I might not live. This is often how we feel when darkness comes—that our life is being threatened. We may feel trapped. I couldn't run from the situation of the shock episode. Darkness is much like this—we feel stuck. It is difficult to accept that in staying with it we could survive. Can you, have you, or will you survive the dark experiences of your life?

I survived. In the dark, on my neighbor's extra bed, trying to breathe, I discovered in the dying another way to breathe. Stillness in the dark allowed me to be directed in the darkness. I couldn't breathe through my nose or mouth, but I remembered that skin could breathe. So I imagined breathing slowly, a kind of breathing that did not have an inhale or exhale. It was an inner breath, air moving by means of whatever causes the heart to pump. I accessed the breath and my heart in the dark unknown through my body. In the deep abyss beneath the waters, I didn't perceive dying as a bad situation. It was just a situation. Is a dark experience a situation we can survive if we stay awake and not perceive the situation as terminal?

I stayed awake to the dying and studied what was occurring despite my fear. In the stillness, in the dwelling, I fed on the life energy that was left in the darkness of dying. The next day, I went to the nearest clinic alone, because I didn't know how to ask for help at the time. As I walked down the street, folks ran away and screamed. My face was still swollen and purple in the crevices. I looked like the walking dead. The clinic told me to go to the hospital immediately, so I walked back home and got in my gold Volkswagen and drove myself to the hospital. The hospital attendants rushed me into a room away from others. Doctors quickly gathered in numbers to look at me. One said, "We don't know how you lived. You're the first person we have ever seen to survive a full-blown anaphylactic shock episode. You are supposed to be dead." There was no medicine needed. I had gotten through the shock on my own. I had saved myself somehow. They prescribed a pack of autoinjection EpiPens for future shock episodes, but I never used them, because I realized I could stop the shock with my mind, my skin, my breath.

The shock showed me that I could do the opposite of panic. Prior to the episode, fear drove my thinking at dark times. I didn't breathe like I did in the shock episode. I wasn't aware of my body when anxiety rose and I went into shock about things in my life. Being forced to dwell in the darkness of an impending death, I realized I had been in shock all of my life and had been trying to survive it.

Darkness thickens when you want to change your life at the core. I wanted transformation. I'd been stressed in the process of moving from my hometown to San Francisco. Although it was an exciting adventure, I was frightened and filled with grief. Leaving my family and familiar surroundings was a great loss. While I knew I would someday leave, the reasons had shifted from superficial to purposeful and then back to superficial. Overall, I yearned to survive the darkness of my life through transformation. I no longer wanted to suffer.

Transforming through suffering plunges you deeper into darkness so that you can open to it. In the dark experience of shock, the mystery of transformation was unlocked. Without the descent, the darkness, I would not have discovered that there is a way to stay alive through horrific experiences in which you know you are dying, literally or metaphorically. There is a way to stay alive in the suffering life brings. We *can* use the suffering to access awareness. Where was I going when I left for San Francisco? I was coming to myself, answering a call of transformation.

Since we feel the shedding away, dark experiences can make it seem as though we are losing something when it may be that we are transforming. We are going beneath the surface of life, diving deep, while increasing our inner vision. We often miss recognizing transformation in the dark as a spiritual experience when we attend to our fears. An understanding of the darkness as transformative might help reduce, if not eliminate, those fears.

Haven't you lived through your dark experiences? What changed in you? Take the time to reflect on the times you survived. Where were you mentally, physically, and spiritually? At some point, maybe you will want to write down a response, maybe not. Keep asking yourself these questions.

Unexpected Descent

Mami Wata is known for pulling folks down into the deepest water. They say some can be attracted by her beauty. In other words, darkness can have an element of seduction. We can be attracted to it, not be conscious of the attraction, and be in the perfect position to be taken down into our deepest experiences. The desire for transformation and healing can lead us to peaceful water in the form of retreats or being with healers we hope can help us. Then, right when we expect serenity, Mami Wata reaches up, grabs us, and takes us down to the bottom of the water, to die or learn to survive.

I met a medicine woman with Mami Wata energy. I'll call her Buchu. Over the phone, she said in her Ghanaian accent, "When you can find out about those who came before you, those you carry in you, then you will understand your suffering and how your family lineage suffers." Then she asked me, "Do you want to do a ceremony around your ancestors? Do you want to find out the ancestral cause of your suffering?" I accepted the invitation with great enthusiasm. I didn't ask any questions about what the ceremony entailed or how much it would cost. She said we would spend the night dreaming. Sounded wonderful.

On the eve of Thanksgiving, I arrived with my overnight gear at the house in which the ceremony would take place. The owner of the house helped me through the door. I looked back at my ride as if to say, "Wait for me," but I have never been one to turn away from what

I bring into my life, even if afraid. I had agreed to walk through this new portal, again seeking to change the suffering in my life. I said to myself, "Move forward." I sat on the sofa dressed in white, arms filled with gifts to the ancestors, while Buchu and her assistant looked me over. "Put your offerings on the altar," Buchu said, and she waved her hand toward an altar filled with their offerings towering at least three or four feet high. It must have taken them all day to erect such a shrine. I added my tropical fruit, tobacco, sage, fine Japanese handmade sandalwood, hand-rolled cigars, and three hundred dollars—symbolizing the exchange of energy between the ancestors and us. When I sat back down, they were still looking me over.

Buchu asked, "Where are your people from?" She was a tiny woman, much younger than me. She squatted in front of me as if we were in an African village chatting each other up. The room had little light, so I could barely see her. She blended in with the dark room.

"Haiti by way of Louisiana," I answered. "Manuel is a last name in Portuguese, so I feel perhaps my people are from Haiti, where King Manuel of Portugal dropped off many of the Africans he enslaved."

"Haiti!" Buchu said, and she went from squatting to sitting flat on the floor. For the first time, with the candlelight on her face, I saw that she was at least twenty years younger than me. I had always felt a medicine woman should be at least twenty years older. Her assistant shook her head repeatedly, saying, "Haiti. Um . . . it's going to be a long night."

I was confused. Long night? I looked around the room. Another person was also supposed to arrive but was late. I wished she would come through the doors right then so we could begin the ceremony and I could settle my nerves.

The assistant said again, "Haiti . . . it's going to be a long night." She looked me up and down. "Don't worry, I'll take care of you."

Take care of me? That's when I looked down and saw a bottle taped up so that what was in it remained hidden or protected. I then noticed the windows were covered up. Suddenly, I realized I had unknowingly come to a plant medicine ceremony. Buchu laughed and said, "Yes. Didn't I tell you?" No, she hadn't. I had agreed to attend in order to better know my lineage of suffering so that I could understand

and transform it. Why wouldn't I want to heal the hurt that lurked beneath my dark skin and had nearly driven me mad and sometimes threatened to kill me? Again, the desire to attend to my suffering had led me to choose the unknown, to choose darkness, to sit at the water not knowing Mami Wata would snatch me and take me below. Perhaps you have been in a similar situation in which you were suffering and, in the end, it seemed you chose more suffering to transform the suffering you already had.

I wasn't expecting to take plant medicine. I let out a slow stream of air. The assistant was almost laughing as I tried to regroup. I had consented with great enthusiasm and willingness to dive into a ceremony to see and speak with the ancestors who were only bones, if not complete dust. I couldn't just jump up and grab back my offerings. There was no turning back for the transformation and healing I had requested. I wanted to explore the dark core of life, see the lineage of suffering in me. I was slipping down a high slope while sitting in front of the altar.

As with many spiritual quests in my life, I never measure the journey beforehand. I hardly ever contemplate thoroughly the reasons for doing something out of the ordinary. I don't want the results of my research, my questioning, to stop me. Therefore, my affirmation and agreement always come before any rational thinking. I had heard people say, "Only a fool would give their money to a healer they don't know." I could have been a fool or not. I was being called to the moment, perhaps before meeting Buchu, probably since the first time I wondered, "What is this suffering?"

The healers offered a full cup of an elixir made from a vine found in South America often called Grandmother. It was dark, thick, and harsh in taste. I had to breathe hard to keep the medicine down. I returned to my seat. The other participant finally arrived and was ready to take her portion of medicine. She seemed calm.

We sat together, still and silent, waiting for the medicine to assist us in the dark. We listened to Buchu singing. Prayers were going down in the dark living room where the windows were covered so that no light could come in from the outside and nothing outside could enter the ceremony. We were to dwell with our bodies, minds, and spirits in darkness.

The other woman began to lose control of herself. She moaned and cried. They carried her in and out of the room many times. I was still sitting upright and quietly listening, still in control. Or so I thought. Buchu asked, "Are you having any visions?" As I calmly replied no, I began to see sweet eyes, sweet smiles, and inviting faces of darkness. The sound of a rattle sent chills through me. I thought I felt the assistant sitting next to me, patting my back, hugging me every now and then. I reached for her hand in the dark, but she wasn't there. No matter how wide I opened my eyes, it was still dark. I had been taken down to where Mami Wata lives, so to speak.

As I began to see from a place beyond, the darkness felt like a blanket of protection. It helped me surrender to what might be in the dark while struggling to see, receive, know, and understand. Like a veil, it covered my doubt, confusion, and fear, enabling me to move through the dynamic sea of blackness called life. It was not the assistant holding me and patting me on the back. It was the darkness.

Time passed, and I heard the voice of a Native American chief humming to Buchu's songs. Buchu hushed me. I was surprised the humming was coming from me. I felt as though I was the Native chief, humming to the songs with my daughter, Buchu. A loud rumbling of buffalo running began at the back of my head. I looked for them in the dark. There were none. I began to talk, but Buchu quieted me again. That's when I saw my mother.

She stood in a circle of men and women dressed in ritual regalia. Skulls were piled high at the door of a hut. My mother reached for me and beckoned me to enter the hut. I shook my head. I looked at my mother over again and again. Was my mother a mambo, a priestess of Vodou? She beckoned again for me to enter the hut, where there was a throne for me to sit on. She said, "Go sit. It is your throne." I knew she would not be satisfied unless I went to sit down. I obeyed.

Hanging on the dark walls of the hut were silver weapons of all sorts—small, sharp knives, machetes, and odd metal tools. I looked out from the seat of the throne. I couldn't hear the people singing or dancing. I couldn't see my mother. When I looked out into the sky, I saw the whole universe. The sky stood still, and every kind of living being on the face of the earth passed before me; trees, animals, and people from all over the world were moving faster than light. I saw the sun stretch into a beam and regain its circular shape. Overwhelmed, I jumped up and ran out of the hut. My mother said, "But the throne belongs to you." I looked back at the hut and shook my head. I didn't want it.

I returned from that vision exhausted. I physically purged what needed to come out of my body. Everyone slept on the floor near the altar until midmorning. I awakened and lifted my head to reacquaint myself with the ceremonial room. The dark papers had been removed from the windows, and the sunlight was shining in. I had spent the entire night on the floor, sitting or lying down at times. I squinted. I wasn't ready for the sun. Buchu and her assistant asked me to come to the backyard after I washed my face and brushed my teeth. I stood up. I felt as soft and light as a blade of grass. I left a ton of old suffering on that floor. In the dark, I had seen my mother in a way I had never imagined. I felt her to be a medicine woman and felt she was trying to get me to see the same about myself. In the dark, my view of my life and my mother's was expanded beyond the suffering between us that often occurred.

I learned in the dark, through this sacred descent, something beyond my knowing. I understood the inherited darkness that we all have and how dark experiences expand one's perspective of life and death. We are led to deep waters in which we can navigate darkness no matter how much we are suffering. Darkness teaches us expansion as we descend into it personally and collectively.

Often, we choose descent when we are searching for ourselves, despite the fact that life has its natural descents, such as loss, grief, illness, and death. Then you choose something to help you with the descent; a healer, a spiritual retreat, or something like a medicine called Grandmother comes along and takes you further down. We might discover that life itself is a descent from birth to death. We are constantly placed in blinding situations with darkness for reasons unknown . . . until revealed.

What have you chosen in life that you experienced as a descent or something that swept you away? It could be a relationship, a practice, or an adventure. What motivated you to come to the edge of the water and be eventually taken, even if you didn't see it as such at the onset? Take some to reflect on the unexpected. Do you trust darkness as a place of revelation, as a place to do spiritual work? There is no need to do a medicine ceremony in order to be undone. Life provides the darkness needed. Are you willing to stay in the darkness of life until you are revealed to yourself?

The Dreamworld as Opening to Darkness

We descend in our dreams in the dark, whether we remember them or not. In the dark, asleep, we lose the little control we have in our waking hours and fall into an unknown blackness. In dreams, visions appear without an explanation. Waking up and trying to explain them is to lose the transformative process of the darkness upon the body. I speak of dreams only if their message was clear to me, if the words conveyed were clear, and if it is clear that the message is to be shared. Otherwise, I sit with my dreams for months or years, waiting for them to reveal to me what the darkness has to say. Usually that revelation comes through someone's words or actions or through an event. Sometimes I see the symbols in the dream appear in real life. In other words, the darkness is speaking.

In the dreamworld, one can see the nature of darkness, unaltered by our ideas of it. In the dreamworld, darkness works with you and not against you. In one of my many dreams, I had slipped beneath the sand near a beach community. The more I tried to get out of the hole, the more the sand flowed in. I tried to scream. Eventually, I gave in to being buried and settled myself. The sand turned dark brown and cold. That is how I knew night had fallen. I heard the laughter of children. Suddenly, I realized that I could see the moon and the stars even though I was buried beneath the sand. I smelled food being cooked. But I was still buried and unable to see anything of the world outside. I fell asleep while buried. When I awakened, I was in my bed, resting in peace.

In settling in with the uncomfortable experience of being buried, I came to a place of peace. When I settled in the darkness, unafraid, I didn't die. I rested in the darkness. Since darkness is inevitable, learning to rest in it allows darkness to assist us with our fear of and struggle with it. How can we rest when some of what happens to us is extremely disturbing? In my experiences of darkness, where there was harm, no matter how horrifying, it was clear that the darkness was a part of life. The darkness was there to aid me in moving forward and to heal the distortions of darkness that caused fear.

At the time of horrific experiences early in my life, I didn't know that I was returning to the darkness I came from. I had no practice of sitting with life, breathing through the things it presented. I was used to running the other way, if only in my mind. Fear accumulated and turned to terror and stimulated old trauma. I often wonder how much of what I experienced and suffered was made larger in my mind because I didn't have the capacity to settle down and see what was really going on. At the same time, I know that what I have suffered, small or great, remains with me as a reminder that I came through each situation. One day I may not come through, and that would signal death. If you are alive, you have come through dark times, and maybe there are a few warrior marks. But it is important to realize that each time you encounter hard times you are increasing your capacity to navigate the deep waters. You breathe better.

Everything is always changing, even the conditions that create suffering. We can freeze in terror, thinking we are protecting ourselves from that which changes and causes suffering, but becoming paralyzed doesn't get rid of suffering. Both good and bad come and go.

How can you find ease in the darkness? Can you see the darkness as a dream in which you are being shown something of your life?

We are fortunate that we have such a thing as sleep. It is the most sacred time of darkness in which much of our healing process, both physical and mental, occurs. Imagine if the world did not sleep. We would vanish. Since sleep is the easiest path into the deep sea of darkness, it is important to honor it as the shamanic retreat that it is. Consider it a time to open to darkness.

You're not alone. We all walk in this landscape of darkness. We don't know what will happen next. We don't know when or how we will die. This experience with darkness is filled with pain and fear, and that can be transferred to anything or anyone dark. How can we open the doors to the darkness that constantly knocks? What is in the mind about darkness that keeps us from accessing its power? What would it take to settle in our life of darkness?

Perhaps we can consider dark experiences as an emergence—as you being pushed to where you need to be. Unless you are truly in a physical dying process, one in which your final death is imminent, be assured that you are not physically dying in dark experiences. You are being shown how to walk this dark earth. There may not be any clear instructions. So that dwelling in darkness, without negative or positive perceptions, will widen your willingness to establish a relationship with life itself.

It is important to develop a capacity for a lifetime by taking in darkness and working with it as medicine. Have you honed your energy? Have you stopped the busyness of life to rest in the womb of life?

We live mostly on the surface, until something drastic comes along—the loss of a loved one or job, a life-threatening illness. This is Mami Wata energy. We are plunged into the dark. While there, we can't see with our eyes and may struggle to scramble out of it as quickly as possible. It makes sense. There can be an intense amount of pain and fear. These are expected human responses.

But feeling that we can ever depart darkness is an illusion. Darkness squeezes and then opens again—like the pulse and rhythm of the earth. When darkness intensifies, it is begging us to remain with it. We are full and need to sit down and contemplate the birth coming forth from the darkness of our lives. Perhaps we need a day in every week or a particular hour of the day in which we attend to what is confronting our lives. I have sacred days during which I mostly commune with nature, read sacred books, listen to talks by spiritual teachers, and try to use electronic devices sparingly. If I'm with people, I mostly listen to them talk rather than get caught up chatting. I listen to the sounds, and in that there is silence. The silence I speak of is not the absence of sound. Silence is an inner state in which one is listening to life and therefore listening to darkness.

I was guided once to sip on silence as if enjoying a fine tea. Doing so requires very little. It doesn't mean taking a vacation and packing up the clothes and the kids. When silence arrives, simply sip on it for a minute or two and notice how it expands into five, ten, or fifteen minutes. It is not necessary always to wait until you have an hour to meditate, although an hour will enhance and increase the chance of experiencing darkness as a path of awakening.

Dwelling in darkness is a shamanic process in which the mind rests, allowing the cells of your body to transform, all while you are still impacted by what's hard and challenging. Needing to know what this alchemical process is will only cause confusion. The mind's involvement will bring the fear that you are already so acquainted with.

A cave of darkness was provided for your actual birth, and it continues to be with you. It is there to be used and shared. It is there to grow you.

GUIDED STILLNESS FOUR

Wading in the Waters
Working with the Deep Water of Mami Wata
North Direction
Intention to Do No Harm Within Dark Experiences

Take your dharma seat in a quiet space in the north direction. Breathe deeply and release very slowly, as before. Do this a number of times and then begin to breathe in your own rhythm.

Here again, read the blessing as if someone like myself is blessing you on your journey. Slowly recite the blessing of protection below, breathing between words.

Blessing

May the dark waters, from which Mami Wata arises,
come through you
and spread as the dark sea that you are.
May Mami Wata protect you as one would protect
the last drop of water on earth.

Guided Stillness

What are you suffering of darkness in this moment? Pause. Is it a life transition, disconnection from a friend or family member, chaos in the world? Your answer may be the same as in the first three gateways. This is fine.

You are still breathing in and out, but as you might do under water. Breathing in and breathing out, notice your breath. Breathing in and breathing out, in struggle you are awakening, your life is being renewed.

In your imagination take on the appearance of a water being. It can look like anything, with fins, fishtail, gills, tentacles.

Choose whatever color you would like your scales to be: white, blue, black, red, orange.

You are now deep in black water, suspended. Breathing in and out. Notice the small movement of the water nudging you every so often. You are still breathing in and out.

Soon, more sea beings float by without stopping. You notice them. You notice their colors. You notice their different sizes and smells. You breathe. There is nothing to do but be suspended in the water for now.

In time, you are approached by an unknown sea being. Its shape and color are different from yours. It's moving fast, causing you to spin around, making it difficult to remain where you were in the water. You begin to suffer from the discomfort of the spinning.

It comes closer. You are ready to attack, but it's much larger than you. You continue to be suspended in the water, even though it is swirling around you and moving you about. You may feel your life is threatened.

The larger sea being comes closer to your eyes. You see it. What is your body doing? Are you rigid or relaxed? Are you breathing? What is happening to your heartbeat? Keep breathing. Breathing harder and louder, but slowly.

Still suspended in waters, you realize the experience of spinning in the water is an old one.

Breathe. Notice this old experience of spinning. Is there fear? Are you wanting it to stop? Breathe in and out.

Challenge yourself to remain in the spinning water. Breathe.

Are you suffering the spinning, or are you suffering the sea being? The being has done nothing but disturb the waters around you. And you have done nothing to the being.

Breathe in and out. See the spinning as coming from inside you, from an old place. See the spinning not being caused by your current suffering, because it has been inside you for some time—before you saw the larger sea being. The spinning lives inside you, ready to be set off at any time.

Keep breathing.

No one to blame for this suffering, even though there is another being in the water near you. No one to inflict harm upon. Has the experience of spinning been with you throughout your life? Are your eyes open or closed?

Look out into the vastness of the water. Even though you are spinning, do the best you can. Notice the other sea beings floating by. Notice how big the sea is. Notice that the spinning is happening only where you are. If the spinning is being magnified, notice if you feel some leftover fear or terror from past dark experiences that resemble the one you are currently in.

Continue to wade in the water, and do no harm to yourself or others. Breathe.

Ask who this unknown sea being is. Look closer. Is it not you seeing you, causing your own spinning around your dark experience? Would you like it to be someone else or something else that's causing you to spin?

Now dive down deeper into the black water that has been beneath you this entire time. Dive deeper still. Your breath will be with you. You cannot suffocate if you keep breathing.

Did the spinning make you lose track of your capacity to be in the dark waters of your life? Rest below. No looking for other monsters.

Sit and breathe, even if you are still spinning from what you are suffering. Be in this dark sea that is spacious and open, even without light. More spinning will come to your life. Recognize the depth of water in which you can survive. You can go deeper than perhaps you think.

When you are ready, read the following ending meditation out loud, slowly, breathing between each word.

Meditation

I dwell in the arms of darkness.
It holds me in the shock of descent.
I receive the breath it breathes into my life.

I will stay,
knowing ascension is what is being called forth.

Remember in these first four gateways you are introducing yourself into the mandala of dark mothers and ancestors and sharing your suffering at this time. This sharing is the beginning of releasing the burden of life and living filled with darkness from a place of power and divinity.

Take some time now, as if you were watching the current of water come and go. Breathe. Journal. Take a slow walk, but as if you are walking on the bottom of the ocean. Come back to your mandala when it is time to move forward. It could be in the next hour, the next week, or the next month. Stay in the north direction. However, you will now cross down into the inner ring and meet up with Mother Ala in the fifth gateway. Water meeting earth. You will move counterclockwise after being with Mother Ala.

BEING MESSENGERS OF DARKNESS

Mother Ala

Mother Ala, of the Nigerian/African Igbo religion of Odinani, is considered the planet Earth herself. I present her from my research, and she can be differently talked about by the Igbo people. All spirits, gods, and goddesses (the *alusi*, as they are called in Igbo) are in relationship to Mother Ala. With a focus on Mother Ala, the Igbo people are earth based, so there is an alusi, or spirit, for rain, thunder, agriculture, and anything else that the earth brings forth. Mother Ala's name means "ground" in the Igbo language. Therefore, when one is going to plant a seed in the earth, they must first ask permission from Mother Ala by making a prayer. Mother Ala protects the land, and when insulted by those who do not consider or treat the land as sacred, she will swallow them up and take them to the underground, which she also rules. Violations by an individual are viewed as violations by the family and community. Violations against the planet include pollution, climate disasters, and corruption. Even when a violation is committed by one person (such as incest, murder, theft, or suicide), those in the religion of Odinani call for a collective atonement to the earth.

Mother Ala is the source of all who are born. She carries the dead (the ancestors) in her womb until it is time for their rebirth. For this reason, she guards women and children, and she is often pictured with children feeding from her breasts. She also is imaged with a sword to represent protection in the same way as other dark mothers in the mandala. Mother Ala is seen with the crescent moon, representing fertility, birth, death, and reincarnation. The python is often near this dark mother, much like Mami Wata. For Mother Ala, the python acts as supervisor and messenger, so that she is aware of any violations on the earth. Snails and monkeys are also considered her messengers.

In one Igbo story, Kamasu, the first Mother Earth, was destroyed in what they named the blackness of Wa. Wa, to the Igbo, was the sound of the great explosion—the Big Bang, as Western scientists call it. From this tremendous explosion, a celestial womb gave birth to Mother Ala—the new planet Earth that we're currently living on.

In this fifth gateway, Mother Ala holds the wisdom of the ancestors who are in her belly waiting to be born. We need their wisdom to help us navigate darkness. We are to listen to the earth and intuit its messages for ways in which we can see into darkness, just as Mother Ala carries insight and divination of the earth and the ground. With our attention to darkness as Mother Ala, Mother Earth, we are better able to open to darkness, as we all long to be mothered in her embracing power.

At this point on our journey, it is clear that darkness and blackness have been misused and misunderstood. The acts of demeaning darkness and praising light have pervaded humanity for centuries and have sustained a false sense of supremacy among light and white people, while others are made pariahs and carriers of darkness and blackness as if darkness itself were a disease. The brutalization of dark-skinned people and the brutality from pandemics, war, poverty, and so on are calls to awaken within darkness, to understand darkness, and to mend our relationship with it. Darkness has become a scorned beloved. Again, when darkness shows its face, it is asking to be loved—not for what it can give or for how beautiful it is, but for what it has to say.

If the python of Mother Earth is listening, then it is also speaking. If we consider the difficulties of darkness as the earth speaking through pandemics, war, and other disasters, we begin to unbind darkness from a theatrical evil, a string of ghoulie creatures. We can hear the primordial explosion again—the bang, the Wa being repeated in each experience of darkness. Each time an explosion comes into our lives to create more blackness, it presents a chance to create another planet right here, so to speak. We can create another place, another way to live right where we are. We have no need to depart this planet to use or misuse another one.

Whether the call is a loud boom, like a disaster, or a quiet gnawing in our bellies, we are being called by Mother Earth to be her messengers in the same way pythons, snails, and monkeys serve Mother Ala. We are to become attuned to the earth, so that we are all messengers of darkness and not complainers about what is happening with the planet as it changes and evolves for its own survival. In being messengers of darkness, we act in darkness as protectors of the planet, and in so doing we are protectors of darkness and messengers of warning the world of climate change.

We don't know all of the reasons these changes are occurring. We only hope the earth stays for our own use and the use of our children and their children. Even the children are crying out in rage because they fear the planet has been all used up and they will not have one to live on. They want to punish those who came before them. Their collective cry is of a personal nature—a crying for a mother, a punishing of mother—as many young people feel uncared for, unprotected. And many have hope, while others display their public rage with the support of those who also are unmothered and feel victim to those they think are destroying the planet. Then there are the protectors—protecting the earth that protects us—who will show up with swords and flowers, fierceness and love, to sustain the integrity of humanity despite (and because of) darkness.

An ancestral wisdom within us tells us that the world needs saving. We have gone about it without listening, becoming heroes slaying various monsters. At the same time, many have chosen to sit with the mountains and rivers to listen, but without any collective purpose of protecting the planet. And here we are, living in these dark times that have always been here. Darkness doesn't go away. It is persistent. So we are to stop in these times and listen to Mother Ala, as her python listens and watches us.

What can we hear in the midst of darkness when we are fearful, distressed, and feel terrorized by the things of the world? How do we get close to the ground and listen like a snail?

Listening and Seeing in the Dark as Messengers

As I've said previously, since I was born out of darkness into a dark body that had been perceived as bad before my birth, I've lived with the injustices that came along with the devaluing of darkness. I turned toward liberation movements while remaining spiritual and religious in nature. And yet I experienced limitations with religion and exhaustion with injustices. Psychotherapy kept me alive, but the experience of therapy kept circling back to the beginning (as it probably should). In the end, I was left staring into my own face that mirrored the night and feeling that what needed to be understood about darkness and blackness was beyond the realms of what had been created for healing and fighting justice movements. After making specific prayers to no one or nothing in particular, I began to turn toward the darkness. I surrendered to the formidable darkness that was never going away. I needed to get close to the earth to listen—the ground in which I would one day surrender to in death.

After my first seven years of intense Buddhist chanting, the oracle—the Black Angel cards—coming through a lucid dream was an initiation into divining my life and deepening my intuition. I was being called to mine the vast darkness I struggled with every day. In the arrival of the oracle in the dream, I was taught to live with the burning of being black. More than to be healed or to affirm my blackness, the oracle called me to be a messenger of darkness, to receive what was being birthed from it and what was dying in it. I was called to protect the medicine of darkness as a fierce warrior, as a dark earth mother. For decades (all my life, really), I had been guarding the open field of blackness. I discovered that I held blackness as more than beautiful: I held it as a sacred cauldron. In being a guardian of darkness, I found myself wanting to ensure the well-being of black people as dark mothers of all living beings.

Soon after the entrance of the oracle into the world, my intuitive capacity increased, and I was often lost, ruled by my temper, feisty, agitated, closed to my own work in the world, and probably off-putting to others. This is what happens to someone awakening to divine power that is surging through their blood without a hut to sequester in. I had no elder who knew and who also could see in the dark. Where do seers or messengers of darkness go in the modern world to be held, nurtured, understood, and taught?

I continued to walk with darkness in many ways. I accepted an invitation to a vision quest by a medicine woman of South African descent. I sat on the dark forest floor for three days and two nights, fasting and listening to the sounds of wild animals. It was a blending back into the natural darkness and land that I knew in my bones. Returning to the dark forest was to remember darkness, to loosen my grip on the need for light. I have spoken of this quest many times because it was my deepest initiation into darkness. I was changed by it.

After the quest, with its vivid dreams and whisperings of animals walking the floor of the forest, I no longer ignored the dark because I no longer was afraid of it. As I realized then, the fear was coming from my disconnection from the earth and the other animal relatives who lived on the earth with us humans. I didn't know who they were, so I had a false sense of my animal relatives as those who kill and kill only. I began to understand darkness as the place in which to see into life. I made a vow to return to the wilderness alone every week and tap a prayer down into the ground, as I was taught by medicine people. I made a vow to get to know the earth, the wilderness.

When there is chaos, it is difficult to listen to the earth. I invite you to consider listening to the chaos as a portal through which to connect to the earth. Start where you are. If you were Mother Ala's python, what would you hear in the chaos? What message would you bring to Mother Earth? What is the darkness of our troubled lives trying to say about how to create a new planet or new life out of the past? If you were Mother Ala herself, what would be the message of the earth—not the idea of what you think is happening and wants to be changed, but her direct message? Don't write down the message until many months have passed with you just listening for it behind the chaos being repeated over and over in our personal and collective lives. When you finally receive it, the message must be chewed, digested, and become part of your flesh. Messages from a nearly five-billion-year-old planet are well seasoned. It may take a long time for a message outside of your familiar ideology or philosophy to arrive. It may take more than the hour of meditation you have allowed yourself or longer than your dream from the night before. It may take longer than the six-month retreat you are on or the multiyear training for priesthood in any tradition.

Messages have repeated themselves century after century. Sages and prophets have come and gone. Darkness isn't going anywhere, because darkness is life itself. For me, being with darkness in the vision quest meant letting go of trying to get healing or light from it. I learned on the forest floor that the power of lightness was not in my hands. Light unfolded on its own and then receded back into the darkness from which it came. I had nothing to do with such magic.

It is necessary for us to listen and see into the dark as messengers in order to sustain the integrity of humanity. We come from Mother Earth, we are carried in her womb, and we will crawl back into the darkness of her womb when we die. Why not open to her darkness now?

Messengers in the Midst of Chaos

Life itself is a vision quest. Every day we are faced with the unknown as we roam the earth. Whether we experience insight, vision, or wisdom along the way has to do with whether or not we are willing to be lost. We are here on earth without any notion of where we came from, where we are, or where we are going. How do we listen while lost or while our lives are threatened by so many things? How do we survive the imploding of political unrest, opposing views within various social justice movements, and increasing hatred toward one another?

We have served in the dark as activists, peacemakers, spiritual teachers, and healers. We may even have created darkness at times in order to stop the explosion we felt might end the world. The end of the world is this destruction we fear the most. That we will go over that edge because we are being pushed from behind by our own chaos. There was already a Big Bang that brought the primordial darkness from which the earth was born. Why wouldn't there be another and another and another Wa within the blackness?

If destruction is at hand, the protectors of the world—the dark mothers, the messengers—will step in to help and to midwife what is coming next. We can't know what is coming, so we don't know what to destroy beforehand. If we kill something of darkness before we see or know it, we might prematurely eliminate something that was sent to assist us. Remember: everything was here when we were born. We didn't come in and decide to destroy what we didn't like and keep what we did.

The ancient Igbo, as messengers and caretakers of the ground they walked upon, would have offered the land a prayer to Mother Ala before inhabiting it and receiving from it. Here in my country, we do not ask. What if we did ask, in the way of the ancient Igbo, in the midst of despair? What if we asked Mother Earth's permission to live on this planet? What if we atoned for the blood, the sacrifices made in the slaughtering and mistreatment of human beings and other animals? The ancient Igbo might instruct us to communicate with one another about the violations we have made against the earth.

What are the ways in which, in order to survive, you have raked the earth of its riches without acknowledging the land as the source? We have all done this to some extent—taking more than we need. What would it look like, in order to mend your relationship to darkness, to become a messenger of your dark experiences?

To serve as a messenger in the chaos doesn't just mean to speak out about what is wrong in society or what other people should do to make things right. A messenger stands in the chaos, listens, and discovers what it is that we need to know at this time. Messengers lead by burrowing into the darkness, into the muck, and knowing there is no real coming and going, no departure and return. To the messenger of blackness, darkness is home.

Not everyone is meant to be a messenger. Not everyone can fiercely wield a sword to protect the integrity of humanity, like Mother Ala, while also giving birth to humanity, like Mother Ala. Not everyone is meant for such spiritual servitude, just as not everyone is meant to be a python, snail, or monkey. What is being called for are a few who are willing to open to darkness, receive, and love the work on behalf of all. Darkness brings distress *and* beauty. Are you willing to engage the simultaneity, the indistinguishable bond of what appears as two different situations—horrific darkness *and* tranquility? Would you be interested in taking part in an engaged council of messengers? You wouldn't have to go anywhere for meetings or have a leader to call you to the circle. You simply would consider a reciprocal relationship with darkness in your heart and trust that it is illuminated and mirrored. Are you open to seeing into the unknown parts of yourself as a way of seeing into darkness?

There is an old, wise elder within each of us and a young, rambunctious one who seeks to know. Consult the elder within and ask that the nature of ancient darkness be revealed to you. Consult the young one within and ask what is to be discovered in the darkness. Although you might not see immediate effects in your life, simply asking these things will bring you closer to listening and closer to hearing the messages of the earth.

In the snow that falls, the earth says, "Hear my cries." In the hurricane that destroys, the earth says, "Hear me." While there are destructive actions of the dark mothers and protective ones, there is also an exchange of love between us and Mother Earth. Protection by destruction, when we are violating the earth, comes from such love.

As messengers of darkness, we can be separated from this sacred work by fear. Our deep love for the planet will sustain us in the work of listening. We are earth's lovers.

Is our love for the planet based only on what the earth gives? Do we love darkness only if it can give us light, insight, or wisdom? Are we messengers who receive only what we can use? What can we give to the world as messengers?

The Grieving Beloved

If this living and breathing planet did not give, we would not be here. If there were no darkness from which to arrive, then we would not be here. A benevolent love that has no gain is what the darkness is asking from us. It is the loudest message I hear within the deepest turmoil of our lives, both personal and collective.

When the most crazy and difficult things happen in my life, I laugh and then I cry into a deep opening of my heart. I fall into the ravine in which the edges of my life have eroded and the water below is a stream of tears. But these tears are not only mine. They run through me from those who are no longer here. They are the tears of those who cared about what happened on this planet and found themselves exhausted. They are the tears from the ancient messengers of the beloved darkness. We grieve together in darkness. Earth is our grieving beloved.

The poet Jake Skeets once described the stillness of his Diné family sitting around the table. He called this stillness "grief." The following is from his essay "The Other House: Musings on the Diné Perspective of Time":

> Today, I notice, among the newfound excitement of
> working from home, small moments of tense air. These
> small pockets of density last only moments before
> another joke cracks or a sarcastic remark bursts the room

into laughter. My house is composed of three young adults in their late twenties. We are all relatively healthy, except for the existential dread of family histories that include diabetes, high blood pressure, certain types of cancers, alcoholism, and mental illness, which are not uncommon among most Native populations across the United States. These temporary moments, though small, are still large enough to notice in the room. I feel their heft balloon in the room before it pops and plastic ribbons fall gently around us. I saw an article headline recently that said this stillness is actually grief. If grief, what are we grieving?[6]

Skeets writes of his family's storytelling as a form of reimagining time on the Navajo reservation. In his listening and observing the stillness, he becomes a messenger of insurmountable grief. He questions this grief and notices that "only with time is this grief possible." Grief is what we find when we open to darkness. Skeets sees into the darkness of the times and sends a message back to us about reimagining grief that can only come with time. Like Skeets, in the coronavirus pandemic I can see more the ways in which my people are still, but not in the same way as his Diné family. I experience around me a long-winded grief, a timeless grief that is still and reeks of caution. In the darkness of the times, the grief of black folks lies in our intention to love and still find ourselves haunted by various forms of illness—physical, environmental, and racial—all of which can kill us.

As a messenger of the darkness, I sat down and wrote the following poem, "What We Intended Was Love":

What we intended was love
without any direction,
we still intended to love ourselves,
to love those who hate if only to test love,
we tended to the effort
not knowing love.

If what we intended was love
and it turned out to be some kind of mistake,
we tried again despite ending up still on the
other side shouting, *You don't understand,*
it's not that I hate you, I intended to love you,
without knowing how to.

What we intended was a love fest
that ended up a protest, a rally of love,
since love could not be felt in silence
or through the disappointment at you not knowing,
not caring,
that what was intended was love.

We could go on babbling,
to recover the language of love,
to recover our breathing,
to recover sanity,
to rescue love, all this in tending to what we intended,
which was to love the enemy so the enemy
        would know how it felt to be loved.

Had we not tried to love in such a way,
deep in the lie that there was a bit of hate in such love,
there would be nothing left of us,
and what we intended would be lost forever.

In grief, we are more likely to be still enough to hear the beloved earth speak. In grief as in darkness, we are shaken loose from inner borders that cut us off from what we need to hear. The renowned poet Lucille Clifton once called herself a two-headed woman, an African American term indicating she had access to both the spirit and the material world. She was a messenger. Clifton claimed to receive messages about the fate of the world from a group of spirits called the Ones. Here's one of those messages:

> If the world continues on its way without the *possibility*
> of God which is the same as saying without Light Love
> Truth then what does this mean? It means that perhaps a
> thousand years of man's life on this planet will be without
> Light Love Truth. It is what we were saying indeed that
> there will be on Earth that place which human beings
> describe to the world of the spirits Hell.[7]

Clifton is among many who have recorded clear messages and warnings that we humans have violated the earth in ways that we might not survive. We experience great grief in what we are losing and have lost in darkness. In this grief, if given time (as Skeets points out), darkness will turn us inward toward our hearts, for that is the only path of listening and seeing this life. We will hear the same messages over and over until we know the taste and smell of our human nature, until we can act from the wisdom in our bones. When we open to darkness, we face an urgent warning to reimagine how we will live in and from darkness. Hear the earth, our grieving beloved.

GUIDED STILLNESS FIVE

Asking the Earth
Working with Mother Ala's Staff
North Direction
Mindfulness Regarding Our Planet

Take your dharma seat in a quiet space in the north direction for the second time. We have finished going clockwise, ending with Mami Wata in the fourth gateway. We are now going to enter the inner ring to the fifth gateway with Mother Ala and begin going counterclockwise, gathering the ancestors' wisdom. Inhale deeply and exhale slowly. Very slowly. Do this several times. Gradually begin to breathe in your own rhythm.

Be prepared for the blessing. Read the blessing as if someone like myself is blessing you on your journey. Read slowly, breathing between words.

Blessing

May Mother Ala, the earth that she is,
hold and protect you during all violations
that come upon the earth.
May she give birth to you in many ways,
feed you with her abundance, and
carry you in death unafraid into infinite darkness,
back into her celestial womb from where you came,
and perhaps you will return as someone's child
and Mother Ala's protection will be there for you.

Guided Stillness

In your mind's eye, imagine you are getting ready to take a walk in the woods. Before you start, choose from a number of walking sticks left by others at the entrance to the path. Pick one of the sticks. Test the stick to see if it is a good walking stick for you. See if your hand fits comfortably around the width of it.

This stick will act as your Mother Ala staff. Before you start walking, look at your stick. What kind of tree did the branch come from? Give thanks to that tree. What kinds of other trees are in the woods near you? Is there open space, like a meadow? Is there a rushing river or a mountain? Is it sunny or cloudy? You can bring into this space anything you would like. If you have disabilities, you can create whatever you need to take this walk in your mind's eye. Make it easy for yourself.

Take a deep breath and look out into the woods. Is it early morning, afternoon, evening? Hopefully, you can still see your way clearly. Take a deep breath in and exhale. Do this several times.

Now, invite your familiar to join you (the one you conjured up in the second gateway). Ask your familiar to take the walk with you.

Begin walking in the woods with your staff and familiar. If you see any loose stones, leaves, or flowers that have fallen, gather a few and place them in your pocket. You will return them later.

You are walking as a messenger of the earth, as a messenger of darkness. Listen to the earth as you walk. What is it that we are collectively suffering on planet Earth? Pretend for a moment you have never been on this planet before. Drop all the news stories you've heard, the issues that have been presented by the social theorists, authors (including me), political analysts, your neighbors, friends, family, or members of your church, temple, synagogue, or mosque. Drop anything that you or anyone else thinks they know about the planet we live on. Keep walking and shedding these ideas. Breathe in and out.

Listen again. What is it that we are collectively suffering on the planet? Hear the cries of the earth. Be Mother Ala, listening. Hold your staff as you walk. Remember your familiar is with you. Breathe and take your time to see beyond the obvious headlines of despair put out by conscious and unconscious media. Use your breath, your body, your intuition as much as you can. Many things may go through your mind about what or how we suffer here on Earth. If you heard these ideas, teachings, or responses before today, drop them. We already know them. We are listening for a cry we may have missed. It may be a cry we don't want to hear.

Keep walking. Look around you. Have you seen any other animals moving about the woods? What does the forest smell like: sweet, pungent, musty, or earthy? What color is the sky? What do you hear? Keep walking and breathing.

When you feel you have heard a cry of the earth you haven't heard before, stop. Find a patch of ground off the path you were walking. Make a circle on the spot with the leaves, stones, or fallen flowers. Do not stand in the circle. Stay beside it.

Now say to planet Earth, "I hear you." Take your staff and tap the ground once inside the circle you made. Say again, "I hear you." Tap the ground once more inside the circle (from now on, tap inside this same circle). Say, "I'm listening." Tap the ground twice. Say, "I'm listening" again. Tap the ground twice. Now say, "Tell us your suffering." Tap the ground three times. Say, "Tell us your suffering." Tap the ground three times. Breathe. Pause. Notice your breath. Notice what your familiar is doing.

Trust a response will come that is not from your voice or from the voices of others. Seeing or hearing from the unseen is an underdeveloped skill. The intellectual and scientific mind is dominant, which causes confusion and deep polarization.

Now say to the earth, "Help me to be your messenger in dark times." Tap the ground three times. "Help me to be your messenger in dark times." Tap the ground three times.

If you still do not have a response to the question "What is it that we are collectively suffering on the planet?" this is good. If you do have a response, this is good. Dark times are always here. There are many opportunities to walk with your staff and receive messages.

Walk back to the path. Return to the entrance to the path or back where you began walking. Keep walking and breathing. Take your time. Notice the smells, the sounds. Notice your breath. Are you breathing well?

When you arrive back to the beginning of the path, return your walking stick. Send your familiar back into the woods to do its work as a spirit messenger of the earth. Watch your familiar go deep into the woods. In some way—with a bow or simply with hands on your heart—express your gratitude to the woods and to your familiar. Turn and leave the woods.

How do you feel about listening and asking the earth for what it needs? You can return to hearing only the voices of others, or you can include a process such as this to hear and listen for yourself. It is possible you might discover an alignment with the other voices. This work can also be done in an actual woods or park.

Make your way home back to your heart and body. Make your way home to the dark earth that you are made of.

Slowly read the meditation below, but not out loud.

Meditation

I know the darkness of my beginnings,
And I ask the beloved earth if I may stay on this home,
offering my heart and tears as sustenance,
planting seeds in right time and place,
with right understanding.
I am your messenger,
being guided toward your laughter and weeping.

Pause and recognize your life as a messenger. Look out the window. Go out and smell the air. Come back when it is time to move forward. It could be the next hour, the next week, or the next month.

When you return, go to the west gate in the mandala and greet Papa Damballah.

DARKNESS AS LIGHT

Papa Damballah

Papa Damballah is the great white serpent in the Haitian and West African spiritual traditions. Again, this spirit may not be recognized or served by all practitioners or priests and priestesses of particular traditions, especially in the way I have researched him. First, he is known as a father figure and creator of life—the god of gods. Here, as creator of life, I feel him to be like a dark mother, as he represents the wrath of the god that burns and purges like the other dark mothers. I am particularly bringing in Damballah La Flambeau energy with his inner heat or fire within the soul. Damballah is spirit, and he carries the Hindu kundalini (life force) fire of the feminine. He is pictured as coiled or circular and works closely with the goddess Ayida Wedo, bringing male and female qualities of life together into a oneness of tension and union. Damballah brings fertility, like a mother, and lives in trees near water or springs. He can reach back to ancestors whose names have been forgotten. He also reaches back to the source of all life that has no gender, race, or ethnicity. Everything that is born comes from Damballah. He is darkness represented in white and light.

The entrance of Damballah into this exploration of darkness (and particularly Damballah La Flambeau, the snake spirit with a flame or torch) is meant to help in expressing the relationship of lightness to darkness, whiteness to blackness. In this gateway, the relationship of darkness and lightness is held by the tension of the fire Damballah carries and within the silence and comfort with which he carries it. In this gateway, we begin to open to light shaped by Damballah, shaped by the source of life and therefore by darkness.

You light seekers can relax. You may have been waiting since the first gateway for the light of this work to be displayed in an explicit way. I have kept you in the dark. However, this darkness will continue while I discuss light from a more integral and often unexpected discourse around darkness. Could it be that the light we yearn for is nothing but a mirage in a desert of darkness?

Prior to writing this book, I noticed my bedroom was mostly white with some black. I wondered about this intense desire for whiteness, as my previous bedrooms had color. I wondered what it meant. At first, I presumed it was a strong need for light. Later, I remembered that in both African and Japanese traditions, white is the color used for death. At an advanced age and edging toward the end of life, I thought maybe that was the reason my room had white curtains, white bedding, and white furniture. I began to write this book on darkness mostly from my white bedroom and mostly in the dark mornings.

Midway in the process of writing, Damballah, the white serpent, revealed itself in both dream and divination. I struggled, because I have such a strong relationship to the dark mothers and have seen them only as female. Plus Damballah was not communicating with me in the way the other dark mothers seemed to. Later, I discovered that he does not speak. He hisses and whistles. Therefore, I had to listen to a wordless call and allow the entrance of Damballah and not force my desire for only dark mothers who were female to prevail. I didn't let the gendered aspects of deities or spirits turn me away from Damballah. In this case, for me (and perhaps only for me), Damballah is both mother and father together, and neither of them, too. It is one creator. Damballah as the source of life is all genders, *and* he is beyond gender.

I am also holding Damballah as a dark deity in the sense that he burns and purges to destroy what needs to be destroyed through the transformation of fire. This quality of destruction yet reformation is much the same as the character of all other protectors of darkness I have described throughout this book. As we see in disasters, pandemics, and corruption, darkness brings light upon darkness. I have forced you to remain with darkness so far, in part because we cannot talk about light without talking about darkness. Know that the darkness gives light, we don't create it; we don't conjure light. Light must be birthed or revealed. We don't know what light is available or what will be uncovered in the light. And we are not as sure of the light as we are of darkness. In this unknown, light is darkness and darkness is light.

As many of us know, there is no light without darkness and there is no darkness without light. But what kind of light are we speaking of? Does the light we experience come from darkness or from the mind?

How can we know? Is it possible that we don't know light or the kind of light that comes from darkness?

We are shaped by the dark, and within the darkness light is said to exist. In the sense of the spirituality of darkness and blackness, light is not extracted, but appears in our everyday dark experiences—sometimes without us knowing it is there. This light is not joy, happiness, or cheer, although we may experience such when we think light is revealed from darkness. Mostly, we cannot see the light shaped by darkness or darkness shaped by light with our eyes. Light is obscured in darkness for a reason, making it difficult to know and access at will. What is taking place is veiled to us, or else we would try to imitate what we think is being done in the dark and manipulate an unveiling in order to have the light we crave.

What is the light? Have we chosen a kind of light we have defined in order to deal with our dark experiences? Is there a light that is as ever evolving as darkness? Is light more than a companion or result of darkness? Is the light the dark itself, momentarily perceived as light?

Perhaps we can understand darkness as light when we consider death as life and life as death. Are we not dying as we live? There is not life alone, as there is not light alone. So when yearning for light, we also long for darkness. The alchemical process of shaping darkness as light is what we are learning each time we are faced with dark matters. Therefore, dark experiences that rock our world are the experiences of light as well. The one is the other. In troubled times or with troubled people, we experience the dynamic and constant merging and indistinguishable oneness of darkness and lightness. In this view, lightness doesn't necessarily feel as good as we would like it to.

Our minds make the distinction between light and dark based on what we have been taught. What we experience of light and dark are separated in our minds because we are in a body that discerns things as either outside or inside of ourselves. Most of us cannot access the alchemical process of dark and light or life and death, and therefore we articulate our experiences of dark and light only as two separate experiences—one bad and dark, one good and light.

During the COVID-19 pandemic, people all over the world experienced great anxiety, rage, and grief. We spoke of it. We saw it eating at us. At the same time, there was also another state of being. While in the dark valley of rampant disease in the world, we also experienced the warmth of the sun, the colors of the earth, and the breath of the wind. We experienced new collaborations and a new awareness of one another. How do we live with the integrative, challenging nature of darkness as both rampant disease and the warmth of the sun, as one state of being?

Damballah—a cosmic serpent or sky serpent—is said to have created everything out of darkness. His specific power is to energize or germinate that which is dormant. This powerful energy, while represented as fire, is in my view exactly how I experience light. When I am energized, usually by waking up to something once hidden in my life, this energy is light. It can't be seen. It is not white or bright. It is pure energy. It is physical and spiritual simultaneously. Other than seeing light with our eyes or feeling it emotionally as not being weighed down and burdened (which is how we see darkness), what other ways can we experience light?

Consciousness, Darkness, Energy, and Light

Eckhart Tolle teaches light as consciousness. In my reflection of his view, light as consciousness is a light you can't see. You can't know it from the surface of things. Tolle asserts that without consciousness there is no world. In essence, the world doesn't appear to us unless we are conscious of it. In a video miniseries called *Teachings on "Being the Light,"* Tolle begins with a statement by Jesus, who said, "You are the light of the world, and I am the light of the world."[8] In essence, we are being light, not longing for it to come into our lives. Tolle gives a quick explanation that "being light" is not a social identity. In my words, there is no one person or people who carry the light because of race, gender, sexuality, religion, class, ability, and so on. Yet we often associate the light with certain people or characteristics. We might say, "That person is light, and that person is dark." But we are all the light of the world, and the world is dark. We can't create this light consciousness in our heads. We can't know how to be light until it is revealed. As much as we try to find out how to live before we have lived (repeatedly failing at doing so), we still keep trying to do what we can't do.

To experience the integrative nature of darkness as light, to experience Damballah or the source of life, is to experience the deep mystery of our lives. In other words, light is not an abstract phenomenon we want (or claim we want) at the onset of darkness. Light is realized and shaped through our experience of darkness. Consciousness as light comes from darkness. Light is unknown until we discover it, again and again.

Many of us learn how to meditate to discover the nature of this life. We might start off with merely wanting to be calm, and this may quickly escalate to wanting a teacher to help us remain calm. Soon, we may decide to leave the training dissatisfied, or we might stay and work with the ways in which we suffer. I could feel Zen Buddhism helping me touch the heart-mind. I felt changed after my first three-week intensive retreat. I was unaware of what changed other than that my jaw and head muscles had loosened and my eyes had softened. A friend came on the last day of the retreat to sit. After the retreat she said, "You look so different." I felt different. My friend looked different to me, too. The sound of her voice was not the same as I remembered prior to the retreat. I simply nodded at her observation. I couldn't explain anything.

I do know that the stillness revealed things from a deeper consciousness of myself. Before the retreat, I knew things about my inner world, but I experienced a more profound seeing and feeling in those three weeks. In the end, I was no longer intoxicated with who I felt myself to be. Instead, in the darkness I surfaced in the retreat as light. I didn't see light or know it existentially, but I was conscious of it in my heart-mind. An awareness of consciousness and an awareness of a non-intoxicated self came together and seemed to obliterate all that I knew. In the darkness, I was what I was looking for. You are what you are looking for. In the field of consciousness, you are light and dark during your dark experiences.

When Jesus said, "You are the light of the world, and I am the light of the world," his experience in the world mediated such consciousness that the light was everyone. If we all experience darkness, then we are the light, and there is nothing to long for. In opening to darkness, we are welcoming the experience of being light. Only through consciousness do we know life or the world we live in. Only through consciousness do we know darkness as lightness.

When we see our dark lives as experiencing the consciousness of light, we are opening to darkness. In darkness we begin to experience the transformative process we seek, pray for, or call forth in our lives when we are suffering. We can see with consciousness that when we turn away from darkness, we turn away from the light we crave. In darkness, we see that we are constantly transforming, that we are in a dynamic and ongoing merging and indistinguishable relationship with darkness.

Rarely do people choose darkness over lightness. Our tendency is to choose lightness, primarily because physical light feels good. The sun feels good. A bright full moon feels better than the tiny new moon we can barely see in the darkness. I can affirm for myself that a bright, open space raises my energy. I enjoy the dawn, but I also enjoy twilight—both being dark times of the day. I still hesitate to meet the dark dreamworld, not knowing what will transpire. I know these feelings as having been shaped by experience and mediated by consciousness. However, experiencing the consciousness as light that is shaped by darkness feels deeply transformative and more profound than a bright room. It means living with darkness as a great gateway to knowing life—perhaps before we live it.

Once I died hanging off a cliff. Eight friends and I decided to take a walk on a trail near Cooks Beach in Gualala off the Pacific Ocean, three hours north of San Francisco. The autumn air was breezy and cool; the leaves were starting to fall. We chatted and laughed as we took the street that led to the trail. We passed homes spread out in length and whose yards were filled with trees and fat green bushes. The street ended, and the dirt road began. We could only walk in twos at that point. We were on the edge with grassy hillsides, the ocean moving below and its wind chilling our faces. We continued to chat and walk along the small road as it became narrower. Eventually, we had to walk single file, one behind the other.

The road became more rugged and narrow, starting to decline steeply. We were still high up with the ocean below, but we couldn't look at the ocean for fear of slipping off the edge. Our smiles changed to worried looks. The best hiker among us reached the end of the decline, which led to a grassy meadow and then to the ocean. She jumped for joy, and we all watched her. We continued so that we could have that same joy and sense of achievement, even though the path looked treacherous to most of us.

Suddenly, one member of the group slipped. Her foot hung over the edge. She screamed. Our best hiker ran back and pulled her up. Afterward, breathing through the trauma of almost losing our friend, we all turned back quickly. Out of fear, I turned too quickly. I took a few steps, and I slipped over the edge and died. Of course, not really. I landed on a small ledge below the narrow road, shaking and crying. One of my friends risked her life to come down the steep edge to help me. I began to fear for her life, too. She got behind me and pushed me up, which caused her to slip farther down and almost fall off the cliff.

In the moment of dying, I could feel the freedom of death, but I was unwilling to go. I would not have called that moment of dying light per se, but it was. It was a dark moment insofar as I was possibly losing my life and causing the death of the friend who was helping me. But in the dark was the light of seeing my life as death and feeling the death as freedom. The light shaped by darkness cannot be seen with the eyes—or the mind. The only way to deal with the darkness of death was to simply feel my friend pushing my buttocks up until I could crawl to safety. This kind of light cannot be brought forth with desire. The cosmic and primordial light as in the energy of Damballah was coming through me, as it comes through us all.

Spiritual Paths of Darkness Exchanged for the Light of Progress

There have always been ancient spiritual paths of darkness. Over time, humans perceived them as backward and thought they caused suffering, and so the ancient practices that used darkness declined in comparison to religions that worked in the light or with enlightenment. Paths involving sorcery, witchcraft, and shamanistic practices—as well as the African-based religions of Vodou and Ifà—were attacked for being dark religions. Their shrines were destroyed, and their leaders and practitioners were either wiped out or forced to adopt dominant religions. At one time, Buddhism was not welcomed in the US, along with its Japanese and Chinese practitioners, because it was unknown. I believe that in order for Buddhism to survive, practitioners did not transmit many of the rituals or ceremonies that could be viewed as dark or shamanic. In contemporary times, Westerners praise indigenous tribes of the Americas for their medicinal knowledge, but they see their spiritual practices as archaic or primitive. As the modern world pushes against old traditions, people have exchanged the practices of the dark earth for a life filled with things that satisfy primal cravings but not necessarily the soul.

When we decide that certain spiritual paths are marked with an external evil darkness, are we wiping out, at the same time, rituals and practices that effectively use darkness as a sacred portal? Why were practitioners taught to experience darkness as a way to see within? In a variety of traditions, followers would go into the woods by themselves or be left on a mountain or in a cave for long periods of time so that they would have to contend with physical darkness and the darkness of their mind. Some spiritual traditions require practitioners to live in a dark place for many years, especially if they are being trained to be medicine people, healers, or teachers. In my own spiritual experiences, I have sat in the dark woods and have sat in the dark spaces of a Zen meditation hall off and on over many years, communing with divine dark demons and deities.

The spiritual traditions that use darkness provide a path to encounter the deep grit of life—the ugly and the painful. Devastation and destruction of self or of one's way of living are part of the path.

Adyashanti writes, "Make no mistake about it—enlightenment is a destructive process. It has nothing to do with becoming better or happier. Enlightenment is the crumbling away of untruth. It's seeing through the façade of pretense. It's the complete eradication of everything we imagined to be true."[9] Without opening and dwelling in darkness, you will suffer from what many call "spiritual bypassing" on your way to the light. You will artificially end dark experiences rather than realize that dark experiences end on their own. Dark experiences ebb and flow, shaking us loose every time. Avoiding the dark, the difficult, or even black-skinned people, in an effort to seek out the light is a way of shunning the gifts of darkness.

Some teachers will not accept students who have not walked thoroughly in darkness, who have not encountered themselves in the dark, which indicates they haven't committed themselves to the hard work of transformation. Students who have not done this tend to come to the path with intellectual or psychological questions rather than in the spirit of a quest or inquiry of life. Have you traveled the dark deserts and seas of life until you were completely undone? Have you screamed and purged in the dark? Are you ready to hold the hand of someone who can walk with you and point out a thing or two? We are rarely told that upon entering a spiritual path we will be burned by fire at the door before we meet the water we seek.

The fire at the door is the energy of creation. It is Damballah. The fire, filled with smoke and unclear light, still illuminates what is ancient in us, in the sanctuary, and in the world. We might tremble and run from the dark, thinking that it is the opposite of the light we are seeking. When we do so, we are running from light as much as from darkness.

When spiritual teachers and healers who exalt the light turn us away from darkness, they are turning us away from a vibrant and rich journey of life. An invitation to darkness on a spiritual path is an invitation to light. It is not a light in which you are necessarily awakened, but a light you continue to experience as consciousness. In the sense of its perpetual and eternal use, light is not an exaltation you come to from darkness and then all is well. Light is still the dark. You can't know it or see it, but you can discover it, and each time it is different, just as darkness is different.

When a person experiences extreme darkness, they often misinterpret it as fate or a result of their karma or previous actions. But perhaps this person has been invited into the sanctum of darkness in which they already existed. In essence, a person undergoing extreme dark experiences is in sacred training. What happens on spiritual paths is that they mimic what happens in life. There is birth and death. Does the birth not come from death, and the death from birth? In this view, we are all on a sacred path, with all of its potholes, tsunamis, and other surprises.

When darkness comes to a person's life, they are sometimes accused of being at fault. The person is viewed as *being done to* because of their actions. They may be told things like, "Wow, you have a lesson to learn. Bad things keep happening to you." We could instead view people in trouble as experiencing a sacred descent, a pause offered by divine intervention, or a period of learning to dwell in darkness, which is to dwell in this life.

Usually when we enter a spiritual path, we need to reconcile our relationship to dark experiences, matters, and people. We have been severed from darkness by a number of successful approaches throughout history. As I mentioned previously, our disconnection from darkness has created pervasive terror and anxiety within and toward one another. But more importantly, the severance has stunted the growth of humanity. Spiritual paths that use darkness as a portal are meant to help us in healing our abandonment of darkness and feelings of being overwhelmed by life.

Grasping for Unknown Light

Our efforts to sustain light by turning away from darkness leads to a life with attention paid only to light. With such attention, we experience great disappointment and hopelessness if light doesn't appear when we want it. Those with attention only to light are exhausted by the work of sustaining an eternal glow in and around them. They conjure artificial light by pretending all is good in their life. And when there is darkness, especially at challenging times, folks who carry their personal brand of light will beg or force themselves and others to come into the light and to do it quickly or forever perish.

I want to note again that many need spiritual guidance or professional help to sustain their lives in the face of inevitable suffering and darkness. Even so, teachers and professionals cannot lead you to light. They may instead turn you toward darkness so you can see and discover what is transforming or emerging in your life.

Imagine reaching out to grab something that's not really there. You try over and over, only to discover what you're reaching for doesn't exist in a way that you can grasp or possess it. Much of what we seek on spiritual paths is like this. We want something to possess. Something to take to bed with us at night or hold as we walk through the dangers of life. We look for teachings we can gather in our pockets, and we pull them out when things fall apart, or we display them to others to show our spiritual evolution. And there is the key word: *evolution*. Evolution is the reason we cannot hold what I call *dark light*. Darkness is an ever-evolving spiritual path.

Darkness as light is evolutionary. Blackness is evolutionary, dynamic. We cannot hold that which is dynamic, ancient, and new. What evolves carries with it that which *was* and *is*. It creates that which *will be*. We live in a world of demand and supply. We are trained to give and get. If we give of our life in this way or that way, perhaps we will become rich, talented, loved, or thought of as a spiritual teacher. And when what we have gathered or managed to possess doesn't lead to achievement, we are disappointed with life and angry at ourselves, regretting all the hard work we put into the things we gathered to make a good life.

We do the same thing so that we will receive and possess light. If we "have" light, we feel we can use it for personal benefit, give it to others, or perhaps sell it as a teaching, all packaged up in glowing colors. But this kind of light is not sustainable. We cannot successfully harness light and give it, because it is unknown and ever evolving inside of darkness. I, we, can't possess darkness either, but I don't think anyone is trying to do that—especially darkness of the painful kind.

On clear days when the sky is big in New Mexico, the morning birdsongs fill the air, and the sun is visible everywhere outside. Inside my adobe casita, the sun shines only where there are openings, through a few windows and beneath the heavy wooden front door. The adobe-style home is the perfect construction for a house in the desert. With few openings, it keeps the house warm in the winters and cool in the scorching heat of summer. It also keeps the house dark (although some of the newer adobe-style homes have lots of windows). This was disconcerting to me as a native Californian when I moved into the house. I adored the sun and wanted it to flood the homes I lived in. In fact, prior to living in New Mexico, I would not live in a house unless it was mostly windows. I would set up my writing desk and comfortable chairs near the largest west- or east-facing windows, so that the sun would land on my face rising or setting. I would feel energized and held by such light. The light helped my heart to open and my words to flow as I wrote about life. Sometimes I wrote in the night by the glowing moonlight. In all cases, there was an external light that assisted my creativity. The external light of the sun and the moon drew out the light within me to clarify the dark interior of my life.

But relying upon any kind of light for my creativity meant needing some kind of superficial light to sustain it. When it was time to write, I would grasp for sunlight or moonlight to lead me to my masterpiece. Relying on external light in this way would eventually prove dangerous to my creativity. It was like waiting for just the right weather conditions to come about and withering if they were less than ideal.

The light I really needed was that which was shaped by darkness. Dark experiences were my muse. I held misery close—not to lay it out on the page as sorrow, but to show it as darkness dressed in its finest. Fortunately, with a cup of hot tea or hot chocolate, I write well on rainy and cloudy days or on dark, windy ones, when you can't see the sun or moonlight. In this external darkness, I see into the dark interior of my life; and the darkness provides a cave in which everything inside me has refuge. Some of our greatest visual artists, musicians, writers, and filmmakers have created their most profound works in darkness—from pain and suffering, from illness (mental and physical). What they shared with the world was born of darkness.

Some will say that we need a balance of light and dark. But who is it that does the balancing? You? The *dark as light* and *light as dark* is Damballah—not the god, but the energy of that spirit or any creative source of life. Darkness and lightness are bound together such that we cannot distinguish one from the other. Opening to darkness is opening to light energy shaped by darkness.

In my own writing and visual art, I open to darkness, which is my life. In seeing my life, I am opened to light shaped by darkness. I write from that light—from a consciousness of a lived experience that is dark in nature, unknown, black, and always, always to be discovered. When I write, I am discovering light shaped by darkness, and it is by no means as bright as the sun. It is energy and consciousness that cannot be seen.

If you attempt to grasp the light of these words with your mind, your head will spin. It is nearly impossible to articulate the nuances of oneness in language. For that reason, wisdom teachings were never written down in ancient times. They have regularly been conveyed in stories or by one living with a wise sage and seeing the teachings through their lives. So everything being presented here is meant to stimulate you on your own journey into your own life—even if it is confusing. Why must what you are seeking be clear to you before you have found yourself? Again, patience is key. Take time to settle. See if you can slow down and take in the wisdom that comes without effort. Try not to speed through the book. It took time to write, and it will take time to read and digest.

Darkness as light is unknown, but it can be experienced without grasping. We are learning to trust darkness as light when great tragedy, loss, or destruction enters our lives, personally or collectively. We see so well at these times. We create new paths and carve out new ways to live. Why allow a mirage of light to deter you?

GUIDED STILLNESS SIX

Stoking the Fire
Working with the Flame of Papa Damballah La
Flambeau
West Direction
Effort Toward Light as Consciousness and Energy

Take your dharma seat in a quiet space in the west direction for the second time as we continue going counterclockwise. Take a deep breath and release it very slowly. Do this several times, eventually breathing in your own rhythm.

Read the blessing as if someone like me is blessing you on your journey. Read slowly, breathing between words.

Blessing

May the fire of Damballah La Flambeau
that emerges from darkness
lead you back to the ancestors whose names
you do not know
to create a circle of cosmic, primordial, unseen light
around you—
a light that is beyond human imagination, meaning,
or comprehension.

Guided Stillness

What are you suffering today that you feel others may be suffering from as well? Breathe and take your time as you contemplate this question.

This is both a personal and collective suffering. Where in your body do you feel the pain of the suffering? Don't assume you know. Check in and see. You might be surprised.

Your body is as long as Papa Damballah, the sky serpent. Mentally scan your body, starting at your feet. Check the bottoms of your feet, then the tops. Notice your toes, each one. Move to your ankles, then to your legs, front and back. Then your knees, thighs, groin, buttocks, gut, belly. Pause at each part. Look and see how you are doing. Go up your torso; check in with your chest. How is your heart beating? Scan your arms and shoulders. Notice your neck. Is it stiff? The neck is a conduit of energy from your head to your belly. Is there a connection from your head to your body?

Now, again, find where in your body you feel the pain of your most present suffering. Wherever the pain of suffering is lodged is where the consciousness of light and energy is working in the darkness of your body, mind, and spirit.

Feel this fire in that part of your body. It could be a small burning fire or a large flame. Notice if this part of your body has been gnawing at you for some time. Pause and breathe.

Now see this gnawing—this pain, this fire—as light and energy. What color is your fire? What color is your energy? Where is your energy high, low, or not detectable? Pause and breathe.

As you look into this fire of suffering in your body, say the following mantra several times: "Opening to darkness is opening to light energy shaped by darkness."

Keep your focus on the fire in the part of the body where your suffering is lodged today. Feel the mantra as you bring energy to your body. Continue repeating the mantra until you feel a shift. Things may intensify, subside, or ebb and flow. Are you feeling more energy? Has the fire shifted to another part of your body?

We are stoking the fire within you to bring energy. Stop if you feel light-headed or uncomfortable. Lie down if you need to. We want, not to cause more pain, but to provide more energy. Keep repeating the phrase to stoke the fire within you. This is the use of light that comes from your dark experience.

Breathe in and then make a noise on the exhale. Loudly. Hear the sound of the out breath as stoking the fire of energy in you. Sustain an audible out breath for a minute or two and then stop.

While you may be suffering, the energized light or fire is sustaining you through these dark times.

Now you will send this energy to your mind and spirit. Say this mantra: "I am the consciousness of the light that comes from darkness."

Repeat the mantra several times, at least until you feel your body has been fueled with more energy. To engage the transformation of suffering, energy is required. Rejuvenation is possible here.

After chanting the mantra, stop and then inhale and exhale with a rush of air from your body. Repeat this at least three times.

Now, please read slowly the following meditation before moving along.

Meditation

I trust the darkness for the light it is giving at this time.
I know the darkness is filled to the brim
and I need only be aware
of how it generously overflows into my life
for the sake of wellness.
May I be ready and willing, even in pain,
to let the unknown light show me its face.

Pause and breathe without trying to reach back to an idea of light. Notice any remaining fears or terror of the dark and your strategy to end it. Rest a bit before moving on. Come back when it is time to move forward. It could be the next hour, the next week, or the next month. After this gateway, be prepared to greet Mama Erzulie Je Rouj in the seventh gate.

SEVENTH GATEWAY

UNDERSTANDING "EVIL" AND DARKNESS

Mama Erzulie Je Rouj

Mama Erzulie Je Rouj (Erzulie Red Eyes) is considered a violent spirit in Haitian Vodou. She is not necessarily a spirit that all Haitian Vodou practitioners know or acknowledge. As I said earlier, a high priest and priestess of Vodou are called to their own particular spirits. I had never heard of Mama Erzulie Je Rouj, but finding her story as I was writing this book caused me to include her because her image was difficult to take in. She is truly a wrathful mother. She is related to Mama Dantor (who is also an Erzulie) but is more ruthless than Mama Dantor's dark side. Mama Erzulie Je Rouj's eyes have turned red from crying in distress and from feeling the bittersweetness of life. With her many swords, she takes revenge. The severed heads in the image represent that which needs to be destroyed—anything that keeps us unaligned with the earth and with our hearts. Like all the dark mothers in this book, Mama Erzulie Je Rouj represents the fierceness that can be experienced in those who are marginalized in the greater society. She protects in the name of what is perceived as going against a sane and liberated humanity. Mama Erzulie Je Rouj arises in everyone, despite race or skin color, especially in activists who are working to bring justice to the world. If we look at rage and anger with the mind of Mama Erzulie Je Rouj, we can see the work of social activism from a place of divine action and livelihood.

In one view, blackness as the twin of darkness is seen as unwell, never healed, always violent, and otherwise without redemption. That view would have us believe that none of us are capable of transformation, liberation, or ascension within darkness or within our dark experiences. But we know that is neither correct nor an authentic presentation of suffering.

When I opened the doors to my own Zen Buddhist temple, along with an image of Bodhisattva Manjushri and his sword, I also was called to place an illustration of Mama Erzulie Je Rouj with her swords on the altar. As a result of my leaning toward Vodou, I brought her in to protect the temple—not to offer outside protection only, but protection from our human tendencies to harm each other due to lack of understanding. We can easily destroy a temple, sangha, or community by exploiting each other for personal gain, by acting from unconscious habits, or by creating environments in which one group is deemed superior or inferior to others.

I also brought Mama Erzulie Je Rouj into the temple because there was a desire among my black students to work on internalized oppression in the context of Buddha's teachings. We were and still are seeking to know how to embrace darkness and to thrive. Mama Erzulie Je Rouj, while violent herself, serves as a reminder that when violence by way of speech, body, or mind arises in the sangha, we need to pause and contemplate the peace that is available in our hearts. Her image helps all of us to remember that even when we have turmoil within us, perhaps we could direct our feelings of revenge to protect our sacred spaces. Ultimately, her presence helps us recall our ancestral wisdom and remember that our presence together can embody safety, protection, and gratitude.

In this gateway, we face the evil nearly always associated with darkness and blackness. We begin to see how what we call evil interacts with our experiences of the dark. Here we are considering something different: that evil, demons, and even Satan have lost their purpose and role in the growth of humanity. Let's walk with the protection of Mama Erzulie Je Rouj, who knows the world of evil. Allow the familiar you chose in the second gateway guided stillness exercise to be with you. You can also bring along Mama Dantor and be the child in her lap.

I was sitting with decks of my Black Angel oracle cards at an event when a black man walked by with his black wife. He looked at me, said "Voodoo," and pulled his wife away from the table. It made me wonder if I should put the oracle cards away for another time in life. Were folks ready for the true spiritual power of blackness and darkness? Would they stop and take the time to see the depth of the black medicine I was presenting? Even hearing "black medicine" conjures up trouble for those who have been spooked by others who have misnamed, misused, misrepresented, and dismissed anything associated with black, even black angels.

Most people associate African spirituality and religion with evil far too quickly. Does the association of evil with blackness have to do with the disregard or elimination of everything dark? The man pulled his wife away because he deemed my Black Angels *evil*. He looked upon me as evil, too. What is evil?

When my father died, I called my mother and told her that I had seen spirits in my room and images of Daddy's white gloves that we'd buried him with. My mother shouted at me over the phone. She told me I needed to pray. It was her way of informing me that something evil was happening or that there was something evil that needed to be eliminated in me. Although she never doubted that I was seeing spirits. I ended the call thinking that if the spirits were evil (as my mother implied by her instruction to seek God's assistance), then I wanted them to go away. But that was out of my control. Dark experiences or experiences of suffering are generally out of our control.

I have long disliked the words *evil* and *demons*. They bring the concept of *hell* to mind, the place where I felt doomed to go according to the Christian ministers I listened to. Every time I hear the words *evil* or *demon*, it feels as though someone is throwing lightning at that which they hope to burn. I have felt the stigma of evil placed on black skin, and I have heard the mythical tale that black people are the devil's children and that we should be done away with. When I was growing up in a black church with migrants from the South and the black community in general, you would be admonished for giving someone the *evil eye* (looking at someone as if you wanted to kill them). I have heard people call others evil despite skin color, especially elected officials. It always seems as though evil people are uncontrollable and that they can and will destroy everyone and everything good. Evil and its hordes of demons are described as strong (if not stronger than God). Why else would someone drag their wife away from black medicine? I don't think they would do the same if black medicine were considered divine and if it had been historically associated with goodness and God.

In *Womanist Ethics and the Cultural Production of Evil*, Emilie Townes writes specifically of the cultural production of evil in regard to presenting black women as morally depraved.[10] With her black womanist lens, Townes defines *cultural evil* as a set of romanticized images and stereotypes that originated in the imagination of white consciousness (a consciousness of superiority) and thereafter was transformed into cultural tools of disrespect and degradation.

In your life, from whose imagination does evil originate? Toward whom is this evil projected? Is the popular use of the term *evil* culturally produced, and if so, for what purpose? Take some time to consider these questions before moving forward.

We haphazardly use the word *evil* when we don't know what else to say about a situation or a person who appears to cause harm. Thoughts, ideas, or traditions that involve violence are considered the product of evil thinking. The meaning of *evil* can vary according to who it will benefit or how it will influence others. What is evil to one person is not necessarily evil to another. As a matter of fact, we don't have a definitive explanation of evil. We constantly reenact an old battle of good and evil, without knowing what evil is other than a feeling or perception we have about something or someone. We even use our irrational ideas of evil to judge and destroy people and things that we may need in the long run. What does our idea of evil do to the fabric of humanity? When we deem someone or a group of folks evil, do we create an invisible prison around their lives?

Evil Is as Evil Does

If evil exists in and as darkness, what is it? Do we open to evil in the process of opening to darkness and blackness? What are we saying when we decide that darkness and blackness are evil in general?

When we try to understand the various atrocities and horrors, such as genocide, slavery, mass murders, police brutality, and government corruption, we often land on the word *evil* to describe these things. Are we talking about morality? Are we talking about a deep conditioning of all human beings? Or are we talking about evil as an existence in and of itself—an objectifying tool to demean something or someone?

Do the demonic and evil aspects of darkness exist, or have we only imagined them into existence? Is it dangerous to open to the absence of light if evil is welcomed in as well?

Bayo Akomolafe, a teacher of Yoruba traditions, speaks about the origin of libations from the Egyptian or ancient Kemetic tradition.[11] Ra, the god who ruled the sky, earth, and underworld, was drunk on the side of the road. People walked by making fun of him. They asked, "What kind of god are you?" This happened several times. Each time, Ra would storm back to heaven, furious. He complained to his daughter, Hathor (also his wife and mother—all in one person), that he was done with human beings, that he was tired of them making fun of him and not worshipping him as they should. Hathor promised to take care of it. She went down to earth and left no stone unturned, but she did her job too well. She tore people apart limb from limb, leaving puddles of blood in her wake and lapping up the blood as she went. No one could do anything about it. Ra tried to get Hathor to stop, but she wouldn't.

Eventually, Ra came down from heaven with a plan to trick Hathor: he and his assistants would pour red wine on the ground and deceive Hathor into drinking it. She would become drunk and forget about decapitating all of humanity in his honor. The plan worked. Hathor was overwhelmed, drunk on the wine she believed to be blood, and she finally ceased her vengeance. Even today, Akomolafe says, the tradition of pouring drink upon the earth (libation) is to deceive destructive forces as practiced in West African communities. They also offer libations for safety, for protection, to give thanks, and to keep evil at bay. In this African diaspora, there are many other meanings for pouring libation, such as acknowledging the ancestors and sharing drink.

For the sake of this work, let's look at pouring libation in Akomolafe's African tale. The libation doesn't wipe out evil; it feeds the demon (Hathor). She has gone over the edge—crossed the line, so to speak. However, Hathor's evil had an important purpose: protecting Ra, the god. We also know too well that using evil for protection can be directed against those we want to eliminate in society.

Gargoyles as part of the architecture on buildings is an example of the use of evil as protection. You may have seen statues, wood carvings, of a snarling Mahakali, Mahakala (a fierce form of Vishnu), or Shri Devi (a tantric Buddhist protector) in what appears to be demonic form at the entrance of Buddhist homes, sanctuaries, or temples. These protective deities are usually black, and their eyes bulge open as if seeing all that is coming. At the temple I trained in, a portrait with the wrathful face of Bodhidharma, a legendary sixth-century Buddhist monk, hung on a wall near the front door. It was eventually taken down because some people feared the image wasn't welcoming. There were also snarling statues of protectors in the Buddha Hall. In the zendo, there was a statue of Manjushri with his sword instead of a serene statue of Buddha in a meditative pose. Manjushri's sword is meant to cut through illusions, including thoughts that might harm us. This symbolic protection in most traditions comes from a shamanic point of view of evil as necessary—necessary for protection from one another, from ourselves, or even from unseen spirits that may not have our best interests at heart.

Earlier I mentioned that deities are created to represent the unseen aspects of our lives. No matter their form, deities carry purpose. So when evil deities are separated from their original divine role as protectors, we lose the connection to the reason evil was created and the divinity in which it was created. Hathor's urge to end Ra's suffering was admirable, but her actions resulted in an evil detached from the divinity Ra expected. Her divine protection gone awry could have been an opportunity for Hathor to teach people about the use of evil as protection. But her rage consumed her, making her choose undivine wrathfulness.

When were evil deities separated from divine protection, from cutting through mindsets that make us suffer, from slaying what needs to be slayed when corruption or harm appears? As a result of evil being separated from its purpose, we came to misunderstand the association of blackness and darkness with evil. Has that misinterpretation brought an undivine wrathfulness *without* protection to black experiences, black matters, and black people?

At this point, you might want to hold on to your idea of evil or what you have been taught about evil. It is frightening to change what we know. But what about embracing evil that has a divine purpose? Mind you, this was a difficult revelation for me. Holding on to evil without its divine purpose is clearly not what we're after. We don't want to embrace that evil. We don't want destruction for destruction's sake. Discerning who and what are evil is important to avoid eliminating the protection we need in darkness.

Let's look further at evil's divine role. Perhaps we can go as far as to say that evil—the word and the concept—may have been invented to ensure constant awareness of harm *and* to urge awakening within humanity. If evil exists, can it be for a divine purpose? What if whatever or whoever is evil is an indicator to us (personally and collectively) that we are at an edge—that we should not go over that edge Hathor crossed? When we are at the edge, we can stop and question: What is this edge telling us? Will there be destruction for destruction's sake, or can we stand at the edge with the protective state that a divine evil is bringing? When we fall off evil's edge, are we falling into the darkness? I would affirm that.

When we think of opening to darkness, does a fear arise that we are opening to evil or opening to allow demons into our lives? Were those spirits at my bed after my father's death actually demons, as my mother indirectly suggested? They did not harm me or seem as though they were there to take my life. What would have happened if I had opened to them as divine protectors sent by my father rather than considering the presence of the spirits as an evil to be eliminated? While I did pray to God, as my mother suggested, I was still haunted by the spirits for at least a month. What did they want?

Wrestling with Demons in the Dark

If we fall deep into any kind of evil, we should be prepared for the existence of demons or at least for those who know evil well. If there is divine evil, there are divine demons.

Demons are often negatively talked about in religion, spirituality, occultism, literature, mythology, and folklore, as well as in comics, video games, movies, and television series. However, demons didn't always carry negative or evil connotations. They were originally divine spirits in some traditions—of the mystery and therefore of God. Medieval Christianity, in an attempt to reduce and obliterate all darkness, made demons evil and stripped them of divinity. As with evil and darkness, demons had a protective role and played a part in reminding us of the edges of life. How does the concept of demons without their original divinity affect our ability to open to darkness? When we run from demons, in what way are we running from our hidden sense of knowing evil and the existence of demons within ourselves?

Demons are often illustrated as human, in much the same way we give human form to deities. They are always us. Some say there are two sides to all of us—the good and the bad, the dark and the light, the shadow and the bright. But these two sides are in one body. We clearly can see opposites in our lives and in the world around us, and yet there is a dimension of life that can't be seen and categorized so readily. It remains in the place of mystery or the unexplained. It is not revealed until experienced. Yet in many religions and traditions it is said that we must wrestle with our demons. These demons manifest as challenges of the body, mind, and spirit. Some might say the holy spirit is what is supposed to save us from the demons of the body and mind. So we seek salvation in the holiness. And yet we do not know completely the nature of spirit; it remains in the realm of the unknown.

So what do we do with demons when we open to darkness and blackness? Do we feed them, as Bayo Akomolafe's African Kemetic story suggests? Should we pour libations for them? Find ways to make sure that their wrathfulness protects humanity as opposed to destroying it? Is the wrathfulness of a divine nature? According to Lama Tsultrim Allione, a long-standing teacher of Tibetan Buddhism, demons (*maras* in Sanskrit) are not bloodthirsty ghouls waiting for us in dark corners. Demons are energies we experience every day, such as fear, illness, depression, anxiety, trauma, relationship difficulties, and addiction.[12] Anything that drains our energy and blocks us from being completely awake is a demon. Lama Tsultrim teaches an approach of giving form to these inner forces and feeding them, rather than struggling against them. Her practice, Chöd, was originally articulated by an eleventh-century female Tibetan Buddhist teacher named Machig Labdrön, and it generated such amazing results that it spread widely throughout Tibet and beyond. Lama Tsultrim has adapted Chöd for the Western world and calls her take on the body-based practice Feeding Your Demons. She offers transmissions of this practice to thousands as a way of opening to darkness, with demons viewed as our allies within darkness. In this work, evil and demons are images within our lives that mirror our innermost darkness. Demons are within us, and we have made statues of them to remind us of our inner state of evil.

Not too many people would ever think to feed demons. Even when we consider demons as internal states, we might believe that feeding them would mean nourishing the worst of who we are. In a psychological or sociological sense, this could be true. However, in the sacred and spiritual realm we are exploring here, feeding demons is the same thing as feeding deities.

Feeding demons requires having a relationship with them. In the African Kemetic story of Ra and Hathor, the relationship between them eventually aided Ra in stopping Hathor from the actions she thought were protecting Ra. In Kemetic cosmology, Ammut was the most powerful demon. She devoured the hearts of those whose wicked deeds in life made them unfit to enter the afterlife. Then there was Apep, who was considered a demon *and* deity of chaos. He was a fierce opponent of light. Kek and Kauket were the spirits of darkness in Kemetic cosmology. They reigned over a primordial darkness, a darkness that existed before the chaotic darkness of pain and suffering. This darkness is that from which the planet and humanity itself were birthed. I touch on these points to return darkness and blackness to their frame of cosmic nature—the darkness before there was an earth, before the sun rose upon the earth.

I can feel the darkness before the darkness of our times. In the quiet obscurity and ambiguity of such darkness, when the earth had not yet been created, I understand how primordial darkness and blackness were stripped of their evolutionary nature. With the onset of particular religions, darkness became the counterpoint to light. Demons were placed opposite deities.

Demons and deities, especially dark demons, operated together to affect the ways in which we live as human beings. Both demons and deities create chaos to help us align with the earth and to protect the integral fabric of humanity. To feed the demon is to feed the deity; to feed the deity is to feed the demon. The presentation of wrathful deities and demons as black by various religious traditions was in alignment with the ancient African Kemetic cosmology of a darkness before the existence of the planet.

Ancient civilizations of Africa grew out of this primordial darkness that included notions of demons and deities. This was unlike the Dark Ages that came later in Europe with the rise of early Christianity or Christendom (the creation of churches and a more politicized Christianity), along with the suppression of scientific achievements and art. These European Dark Ages were a chaotic darkness. They were far from the primordial darkness in which demons were dark deities.

The chaotic darkness experienced today is similar to those medieval Dark Ages. We see the same suppression of scientific and medical findings, censoring of art and literature, government corruption, pandemics, and merciless killing of people sanctioned by government leadership. In this new Dark Age (or perhaps it is merely an extension of the one we presumed left behind centuries ago), demons and evil are out of alignment with any kind of divinity.

It is this chaotic darkness we find it difficult to open to. Why open to chaos? Better yet, can we embrace the fact that we are inside of the chaos, whether we open to it or not? Why create relationships with demons? If darkness is infinite in nature and if infinity itself is darkness, why not? If darkness, demons, or deities are constant, whether you give meaning or attention to them or not, they deserve at least an exploration—not from outside your life, but from within the palpable ebb and flow of life. If we destigmatize the concepts of darkness, evil, and demons and return them to the language as expressions to describe unseen divine existences, then perhaps we can lessen or eliminate the fear and terror of these things or even use them in a beneficial way.

Demons and Dark Deities as Guides

Returning to primordial concepts of darkness and evil allows us breathing room around dark experiences, matter, and people. It is said that Greek philosophers would go to the dark continent of Africa, knowing that it was not dark in terms of being backward or closed to the wisdom of the cosmos. In fact, the Africans were the first to create civilization, including art, literature, math, astrology, theater, and, yes, philosophy. The beginning of African history is not slavery. A dark continent wasn't a bad continent when the Greeks first went to study. They knew the darkness in Africa meant it was rich in resources, including spiritual teachers. Africa provided awakened and transcendent teachings they desired. So they went to study with great teachers of Africa for the sake of discovering the answers to the mysteries of life. We are like those Greeks returning to the source of darkness, discovering life each day and remembering that the journey is often not pleasant. After the Greeks pillaged the African continent and the Africans were later enslaved, the dark continent lost its great sages and prophets. It left only their Greek students, who could write, to transmit their teachings. This exchange has had little documentation, but the influence of Africans on Greek philosophy is evident in the works of Pythagoras and Socrates, who studied with many African mystics of the darkness.

At the same time, no one owns wisdom honed from the earth. Throughout time, people of all sorts have entered the path of darkness to discern and gather ancient wisdom with more clarity and relevance to contemporary time and place. This is how we have recalled that demons and deities can act as shamans or guides through darkness. The presence of demons and dark deities is an indication that the primordial darkness is being clouded by the chaos we humans create. As guides, demons and deities can scare you off the edge of danger by their presence and lead you back into the subtle primordial darkness. How does the presence of divine demons show up in our lives?

There is healing in darkness. The healer in the experience of unsettling times is darkness itself. As with other experiences of darkness, a shaman is not always present to clarify which medicine will surface from our suffering. It was clear in ancient times that the only way to receive medicine for what ailed us was to go inside the suffering, inside the darkness, and let it break down the old and allow a replacement of whatever was needed to heal and thrive. Inside darkness, whether we know how it is happening or not, we can find a spiritual connection to the dark earth, a chance to have our own direct experience of the unseen, and an opportunity to draw upon the wisdom that is available to us. As I said previously, to run away from darkness, demons, and evil is to run away from ourselves.

You don't always need shamanism or religious rituals to access what darkness can give you. We are often led to believe that a teacher or shaman can provide us with wisdom, but the best ones don't provide anything. They lead us to the river of our own wisdom within. The best teachers and teachings are with us in our dark experiences. Hopefully, we come through the hard times full, energized, and open for more.

The darkness of chaos, unlike the primordial darkness before the advent of humanity, continues to evolve as time passes. For example, the evil of anti-blackness reveals the need for justice as well as the need for ceremony within the darkness. Demon deities guide us toward ceremonies for peace, health, and protection. They guide us to the gateways in which we are to actively and collectively mourn what has been lost in the darkness and welcome new seeds in the dark. When we open to darkness, we also open to relationships to all of life, including divine evil. In acknowledging it, we can caretake our lives and one another in a state that is welcoming to darkness.

Darkness is always asking something of us in order to help us open to it. What is it asking? If demons are certain kinds of people, how can we live together with them? If we are nature, then how do we attend to destructive climate changes in the world without feeling we are fighting empty space, without growing hopeless and exhausted? If dark experiences are unwanted, how are we going to learn how to be in relationship with one another and the earth when there is constant chaos? Does darkness come and go, or do we lose a connection to darkness until it becomes amplified in our lives?

There are no immediate answers to these questions. These questions are to be lived as a lifetime quest or inquiry. They are to be held in our hearts as we navigate life in the dark and watch to see if the responses to such inquiries are deep within us—deep below our minds.

GUIDED STILLNESS SEVEN

Honoring the Demon
Working with the Rage of Mama Erzulie Je Rouj
South Direction
Livelihood for the Wellness of All

Take your dharma seat in a quiet space in the south direction for the second time. Take a deep breath and release it slowly. Very slowly. Repeat this step several times. Then breathe in your own rhythm.

Hear my voice reading the blessing below slowly, breathing between words.

Blessing

May Mama Erzulie Je Rouj represent
the embodiment of safety, protection, and gratitude.
May this dark mother's sword help release ideas of
darkness and evil that cause you to suffer.
May her strength join with your strength
to help you survive all turmoil in your life and in the world.
May the wrath of demons and dark deities
serve only to protect you.

Guided Stillness

Hathor was given a job by Ra, but in her effort to protect him, she overstepped. The rage of Hathor can be seen in Mama Erzulie Je Rouj with the many heads she has severed. Remember we are going counterclockwise to gather the wisdom of the ancestors.

Here, we will look at how a livelihood or purpose in life can bring wellness to all. Livelihood isn't just your vocation or employment, but a higher calling of protecting and serving all living beings.

What have you recently suffered in doing your work in the world? Have you suffered invisibility, being taken for granted, stress, mistreatment, or lack of acknowledgment?

Breathing in and breathing out, say to yourself, "I know destruction as protection and as renewal." Breathing out and breathing in, say, "I am aware that I am being awakened."

Let go of all titles and honorifics you use in the world. Right now, you are not a consultant, director, doctor, teacher, minister, artist, social worker, or anything like that. You are not employed, underemployed, or self-employed. You do not earn a salary, yet you have all you need.

What does it feel like to step out of a livelihood built around labor for survival? Pause and breathe.

Now go back to reflecting on the suffering you are experiencing with your work in the world, but without title, rank, or job description. You still do the work, but without names and labels. Do you notice a difference in the intensity of the suffering? Release everyone else in the work story from the suffering of title, rank, and description. Everyone is now just a person doing the work. There is no longer competition, promotion, notoriety—nothing.

Now that you and the others in your work story of suffering are empty of your usual roles, try taking on the divine calling and livelihood of protector. You now have the responsibility of protecting yourself and others for the sake of wellness, but no one else in the story is aware of your new role.

How do you feel as a protector? Do you feel nervous, unsure, fearful, fearless, strong, afraid, neutral, lost? Are you carrying anything to help in the protection: sword, flowers, stones, strong words, sage, spells, prayers, hope, presence, common sense, determination? Do you notice a difference in the intensity of the suffering around your work now that you have been given the divine role of protector? Pause, breathe in, and breathe out.

As protector in your suffering story, what are you protecting for others: equality, joy, peace, access, autonomy, rights, their very lives?

As protector, what of yourself are you protecting: reputation, something hidden, dignity, your rights, your heart? Pause, breathing in and breathing out.

Now access a demon or evildoer in your situation of suffering. Ask the demon to sit with you. Don't worry: you have your protective juju, medicines, prayers, chants, crystals, family, friends, community, and anything else you need to help you feel protected. Pause and breathe.

How do you feel now that you have invited the demon to sit with you? What is the demon doing? What are you doing? Are there any sounds coming from the demon? Any smells? Is the demon looking at you? If not, ask it to look at you. Are its eyes big or small? Is its gaze soft or hard?

Tell the demon, "I know you. I have seen you before." In saying this, do you become more aware of the nature of this demon, this evildoer? What are you becoming aware of? Breathe.

How many times have you visited this demon in the last week or two, in the last month or year? Ten, twenty, fifty times? How often have you been with this demon who shows up in your work in the world? Pause. Breathe.

What do you fear the demon knows about you? That you crave praise, feel unseen, look to be number one, fear your sordid past, your brilliance, your capacity to love, your self-loathing? Pause and breathe.

Continue sitting with the demon. Perhaps meditate together, even though difficult emotions and feelings of anger and rage remain. Hopefully, this sitting together will help prevent you from going off the edge. Destruction may be at hand—not necessarily the destruction for the sake of humanity's ascension but a destruction that brings senseless harm. The sitting is to prevent you from slaying the demon or demons in your situation. Breathe.

End your sitting meditation with a bow to this demon, even though it may not return the bow. The act of bowing is the beginning of honoring this demon for what it has revealed around your work in the world.

If you can, say to the demon, "Thank you." This may be difficult if you don't see the divinity within the demon along with all the hurt it has caused. This gratitude is for your own release.

Next, ask the demon to assist you in dealing with the suffering in your work and to keep you from going over the edge that evil provides. Say, "I need your help."

Now, trust the demon will help in time and depart with a simple goodbye. Breathe.

You may notice feelings of joy or grief because you have had a relationship with this demon long before engaging with the work you were called to do. The demon was simply called in by you, through you. You have been a portal for it over many years. It is neither a good nor a bad demon. It's just a demon of divine intervention.

In a livelihood in which you are a protector, honoring the demon is to honor its divine purpose with dark experiences in which you find the need for protection.

Express your gratitude in walking with evil and demons. Please read the following meditation out loud and slowly.

Meditation

I meet the demons of my own being,
wrathful protectors of alignment in my life.
I see the evil in darkness, not as people or things,
but as the edge in which to stop and turn toward life,
with full attention.
I look, I listen, and I see.

Now it's time again to stop and notice the rise and fall of your breath. Perhaps do no journaling this time, or maybe just jot down a few words that stand out in your consciousness. Try not to block any surprises. Move about. Come back when it is time to move forward. It could be the next hour, the next week, or the next month.

Continue counterclockwise to meet Mama Brijit in the eighth and final gateway.

EIGHTH GATEWAY

CELEBRATING THE DARKNESS
OF DEATH AND BIRTH

Mama Brijit

Birth and death go together in almost all spiritual traditions. In Haiti, ceremonies and celebration of death include an attention to sex, which is illustrated in my version of Mama Brijit above, as death leads to birth. Mama Brijit is not necessarily a spirit that is recognized by all religious priests and priestesses in Haiti, or sometimes there is another name for such a spirit. Mama Brijit is a death spirit and sometimes is known as Mary Magdalene. In my research, she leads the deceased to the afterlife. She loves and cares for the dead more than she did when they were alive. Mama Brijit is said to be the spirit of life, death, justice, motherhood, fertility, cemeteries, crosses, gravestones, women, and the souls of deceased relatives. This goddess spirit of the cemetery is said to have a foul mouth. She is tough *and* tender. It is said she was brought to Haiti by the white indentured servants of Scotland and Ireland, where she was Saint Brigid of Kildare. The Portuguese also celebrated Saint Brigid. Since most of the Africans enslaved by the Portuguese were brought to the Caribbean, this may also be how Saint Brigid became Mama Brijit in Haiti. She is married to the dark Baron Samedi, also a spirit of death, who together with Mama Brijit works on everyone's behalf at death in a fun and feisty way.

Mama Brijit drinks rum with hot peppers, and she is known for her piercing stare. She swears a lot and is symbolized by a black rooster. Roosters for Mama Brijit represent the sun and the dawn or birth and death. They can also symbolize the rebirth that we experience daily. Many folk legends say that the rooster's first cry in the morning makes night ghosts, spirits, and devils disappear. During Buddha's time in India, the rooster was a symbol of warding off suffering, ignorance, and unwholesome states. A rooster (or an image of a rooster) was brought to funerals to ward off evil spirits. In ancient Christianity, the rooster's crowing at daylight warded off darkness and death. So, while Mama Brijit invites death, she, too, also protects against it with her familiar, the black rooster.

Mama Brijit is often pictured as a pale-skinned woman with red hair who is known to perform the banda dance of Haiti in a sexual and sensual way. As I mentioned, sex is very much part of the path of death in the sense of resurrection, reincarnation, birth—or life in general. There are some in Haiti who still practice an old rite in which the first woman to be buried in any new cemetery in Haiti is dedicated to Mama Brijit.

Some say it is through Mama Brijit that the medicine dolls (often called Vodou dolls) came into existence in the Caribbean and other parts of the world. Note that Vodou dolls are not necessarily acknowledged or used by many Vodou practitioners. But it is interesting to consider their origin according to folklore. In the 1700s, many Irish and Scottish women were shipped to New Orleans as punishment for minor crimes and put to work alongside the Native American women there. It is said Vodou dolls were originally derived from the Bridie dolls of Scottish and Irish origin. They were made from scraps of fabric with accessories added. The Bridie doll would be kept throughout the year near the hearth, hung on a wall, or placed near the door as a talisman of protection, then burned and replaced with a new doll for the next year. If a doll was used to harm someone, it was for protection or defense against someone who failed to respect life—which is to fail to respect the dead, as well. The use of the dolls in this way was not considered a ruthless vengeance on another person, as we see in the movies and media. It was a sacred medicine doll that was often associated with Mama Brijit.

I bring Mama Brijit with her fierce protection of life and death into the mandala. I bring her capacity to dance with darkness with an attention to continued life through sex and sexuality. I bring this grandmother to this work of opening to darkness because death is the most infinite and primordial darkness we will all experience. It is perhaps what frightens us most. In opening to darkness, we will find the elements of respect and protection to be consistent allies during dark times and experiences.

The birth, death, and sexual aspects of this dark spirit were the subject of two films with actor, artist, dancer, singer, and costume designer Geoffrey Holder. As a young person I remember that I was mesmerized by this Trinidadian, who played Baron Samedi in the movies *House of*

Flowers and *Live and Let Die*. He was Baron Samedi embodied, and also the well-known actor Carmen de Lavallade was Mama Brijit at the time. While everyone enjoyed these films, many were unaware of the Haitian religious undertone of the work.

Mama Brijit is of Haiti, and she is also of New Orleans, as many Haitian immigrants brought their shrines and practices with them to Louisiana at the turn of the twentieth century. My parents were born in Louisiana at that time, and I was privileged to experience the suppressed religious Vodou traditions through them, even though they were Christians. The traditions were so undercover I feel even they didn't know that there were traces of Haiti's Vodou within them. I wonder what celebrations of death and darkness were lost as many Haitians migrated to Louisiana to become assimilated into the dominant French culture that ruled at the time. However, I suspect traces of Haiti continue in the celebrations of darkness and death in Louisiana today and other places black people migrated to in the years after slavery.

There are many celebrations of darkness and death. As I write the message of this last gateway, Halloween is upon us—the time they say the veil is thinnest between the world of the living and that of the dead. The marking of Hallows' Eve goes back thousands of years in the Celtic tradition of Samhain, when the ghosts of the dead walked the earth and people masked themselves as protection from the spirits (the spirits were masked, too). Later, Halloween was Christianized as All Souls' Day and All Saints' Day. Immediately after Halloween, Haitians and many in Louisiana celebrate Fèt Gede, the Vodou Festival of the Dead. They converge on cemeteries to honor ancestors with rituals and sacrifices for the month. There is also a display of sex and sexuality in the associated rituals and dances, because death is also birth in the Vodou tradition. The first and second of November are also Los Días de los Muertos in Mexico, when colorful shrines are built in cemeteries and families commune with their dead loved ones. The Haitian and Mexican celebrations are not somber mourning ceremonies, but festive times to visit with those who are gone in body but still present in spirit.

These festivals for the dead are also festivals of darkness, though they may not be viewed as such because they involve so much love and celebration. In these festivals, death is an honored crossing. Understanding that celebratory aspect, along with practicing respect and protection, are all part of opening to darkness.

Consider how you felt when you discovered this gateway would be about death. What came to mind? Were you sad, afraid, or grim? Are you capable of celebrating the darkness within death? If not, what keeps you from doing so? If you were to celebrate it, how would you do it? If you already celebrate death, what motivates you to do so? Take some time to ponder these questions before moving on.

Since many of us are not raised in the culture of our ancient ancestors, our sense of death and darkness is skewed to one direction—a narrow place we don't necessarily want to go. Death and darkness are rarely seen as peaceful or beautiful, and they are often not celebrated by those who have lost the sense of ceremony. I feel that is changing. The celebrations that do occur in this country originate from those of cultural diasporas (usually African, Asian, and Latin American) reclaiming the true beauty of darkness and blackness through ancient spiritual traditions. In communities of color, many street shrines begin to appear in neighborhoods where there were road accidents, gang violence, or any public violent deaths. An increase in candlelight vigils occurred in the last two decades. The more darkness of death we experience, the more able we are to look death in the face, as death tolls rise to unprecedented numbers, surpassing those of our largest wars. In fact, I believe that people of color have always initiated ceremony and ritual in the US. The celebration of darkness and death is organic to indigenous cultures and crucial to honoring ancestors, those who came before us.

As my mother was dying, I stared down into her face. She wasn't there, even though she was still alive in the medical sense. I kissed her cheek and saw her in a narrow, tunnel-like portal. She was crouched against a gray wall. I was glad to be at my mother's bedside alone. Even though I didn't want her to leave, I whispered in her ear to stand up and go on. I had seen that portal before in another spirit crossing. There was a deep sense of peace and beauty in the narrow tunnel with rays of lights. It was a place anyone might like to go if they were not dying.

My mother didn't want to leave us, or perhaps she wanted someone to go with her. At that moment, my sisters and a friend came in, and we all sang the gospel songs we sang in church. We brought honor and celebration simultaneously with the grief. My mother left the tunnel. It took me a year to cry in the way I thought I would at her funeral. I could not stop. One time, I was in bed facing the wall and felt someone's hands holding me. I knew it was my mother. I didn't turn to look at her, because I didn't want to send her spirit away. I kept still and continued to cry.

Where she went is beyond me. I can only say that when we open to darkness, the possibilities of joy and peace are infinite. To witness the spirit leaving the body is to come to terms with the nature of our bodies and their inevitable decline and disappearance in death. Mama Brijit's spirit is a reminder to celebrate darkness and know it as birth. Like Mother Ala, who holds the dead in her womb as ancestors to be born again, Mama Brijit holds the dead and honors how life comes through death.

Fear of Darkness as Death

I recently lost a new friend. She died when I was writing this section, right at the time I was obsessing over my own death. Prior to my friend dying, at night I would toss and turn, knowing my life would one day come to an end. As you age, the horizon lowers. Someone once asked me what I would need to hear to make me not obsess so much about death. I chuckled and said, "That I was going to live forever. That there was no death."

Many believe in eternal life in heaven, reincarnation, or no final death. I believed for a very long time that there was no death. This view was furthered in my Zen practice, in which the darkness of death is a continuation of life. I never felt those who died as completely gone. I always felt the presence of my deceased parents, other family members, and dead friends near me. Then, when I was coming out of my first major surgery, I lost faith that folks were still nearby. I lost faith that my beloved ancestors were lingering about. It was a frightening year to live like that, with the feeling that death is final and that there is absolutely nothing after death.

One day my neighbor called me to come over and hang out at her casita. Before that, she rarely said anything more than "Hello." I had another appointment, but I thought, *What the heck, she never invites me over*. I went into her sweet home, and we laughed and talked. We were kindred spirits. Her adult daughter listened in as she walked about the house. I didn't want to leave, but I had to meet up with someone else.

A week later, her daughter came to me across the grass with tears in her eyes. Her mother had been rushed to the ER and placed in the hospital for a week. Now she was on hospice care and actively dying at home in her casita. My jaw dropped. How could someone be so alive one week and be saying goodbye to the world the next? I did a Zen chanting service for her, and the next day my new friend was gone.

But something about her death eased my obsession. My friend had not suffered. Even as she gasped for breath, she looked healthy, and her skin was glowing. I got really close to her face and spoke in her ear. I was not afraid; I was curious. The way she died so effortlessly made dying look easier than the way I had seen others die before. Of course, she was on medication to help, but the glow coming from her was comforting.

The day after she died, I went back to check in on the family. My friend's body was still in her bed. A vision came of the day when she called me over to her casita to laugh and talk. Her granddaughter said that her torso was still warm. The place where her heart had beaten for seven decades was still radiating. Something of her was still there. I knew in that moment that there was *something* after death or that there was no death—that there was just something unknown. Mostly, I realized that darkness had an eternal existence. It didn't matter if I had faith or not. What mattered was that I would be going into the same darkness as my friend had done, and I vowed in that moment to leave radiant and at ease. I let go of my angst. I felt my shoulders drop; my face was as soft as my friend's. The next day I was full of joy for my friend and for myself.

One of our greatest teachers of darkness is death. At times, our fear of darkness collapses into our fear of death. We live with death every day, which is to say that we live with darkness. At times the dying go unnoticed, and at other times the numbers of those dying are so great we can't ignore them and may begin to fear that we will soon be counted in those numbers.

There are different kinds of darkness and different kinds of death, but in my experience it is always a shock when someone I know dies, whether it's sudden or expected. It is always a shock to find ourselves in dark times. What is the shock? That the person is no longer. That they have vanished into the infinite darkness that we have allowed to haunt us. What is the shock of unsettling times? Are we responding to death when we fear darkness? When we are invited to open to darkness, does death eventually come to mind?

The late Buddhist teacher Thích Nhất Hạnh said that there is no need to talk about death, because there is no death. He asked his sangha to write, "I'm not in here" on his shrine. In case the first message wasn't understood, he also instructed them to write, "I'm not out there, either." This is the relative and absolute truth—the truth of the boundless nature of life, death, and, yes, darkness.

How we view death affects how we respond to dark times. We feel we are dying all the time because the horrors we encounter in life can feel constant. What if we were to consider dark times as an organic process of surrendering all we think we need to survive—status, fame, money, a house beyond our needs, new clothes every year, nice cars, or our very bodies? Maybe in dark times we are being invited to consider what we are, if the person we feel ourselves to be will be no longer at some point.

We have been taught that death is the worst thing that can come upon us. We are also taught to view darkness in this way. If you were to tell someone that you are going to die tomorrow or that someone else close to you was going to die, no one would say, "Wow, congratulations. Let's celebrate!" Most of us are taught either that death is final or that death is a transitional phase to an unseen world, although a number of cultures see it differently. For many, death marks a time of moving into ancestorhood, though in some West African traditions to become an ancestor takes years to happen. One doesn't just become an ancestor immediately upon death—they are still impacted by having left the Earth. So death in this view is a slow ascension. As ancestor, one survives and serves the community from a different world. As a result of that view, death, in many African cultures, is not contemplated or spoken of that much, because life continues. The ongoing life of darkness is continued in more darkness—the same darkness from which we were born. Some dance with Mama Brijit to celebrate not only a person's life but also their death. Death is the soil from which more life will spring.

There are many rituals and ceremonies for transitioning into the darkness of death that once were part of the larger culture but mostly now remain in the sphere of religion. A Theravadin Buddhist practice called Maraṇasati ("mindfulness of death" or "death awareness") uses various techniques to enhance the awareness of death. For example, monks are sent to cemeteries or fields where bodies are decomposing to investigate death and learn not to cling to the body. The Tibetan tradition entails a number of transmissions to prepare one for death and darkness, including the reading of *The Tibetan Book of the Dead*. In Zen, there is no death and no birth, because the existence of a self is interdependent upon the existence of other beings and other things. Therefore, when one dies, that former person exists only in the hearts of loved ones who remain alive; the person who has died is no longer. There is no person. Even so, in Zen temples, when senior practitioners or priests die a bell is rung 108 times by various people—one at a time, and very slowly, for nearly an hour. This ceremony marks a time to stop, grieve, and notice the continuing cycle of birth and death.

In my Christian experience, family and friends gather together days before the funeral for what is called the wake, which is similar to how Buddhist practitioners sit with the body of the deceased. But a wake is not necessarily meant as an opportunity to observe death and become aware of impermanence. A wake is for comforting the family and mourning in a more private setting than a church, funeral home, or graveside service. Wakes are also times to eat good food, laugh, and tell stories about the person who has died. At one time, before bodies were embalmed, wakes were also a time to ensure that the person was actually dead before they buried them. Someone would watch over the body day and night in case the person woke up, but also to speak to the dead person and ease their transition into darkness.

The common theme in these death rituals is an observance of the body. In the energy of Mama Brijit, the body is venerated in darkness. The darkness of death is a chance to make peace with the truth that everything that is born (not only people, but ideas, corruption, climate change, and so on) will also pass back into the darkness it emerged from. It is an opportunity to experience the transformation and healing within darkness. While there is sorrow and discomfort with the loss in death, the darkness is present to assist. Mama Brijit is not the Grim Reaper; she comes to help. And maybe the Grim Reaper has a lost ancient purpose in being a companion in death. We never see the reaper's face or eyes to know whether they are foe or friend.

Death has a role. It helps those of us who are still alive to open to the darkness, to the suffering as the transformation we seek in dark times.

Write down the ways that witnessing death has affected your experience of darkness and blackness. Note what insights you gained about death that can carry over to seeing darkness as a conduit to expanding the heart.

We are constantly working to hold on to the passing body. We are ever vigilant at protecting ourselves from death. Despite everything appearing the same as yesterday, the darkness of death opens the mouth of the river of life and loosens our grip on life whether we want to let go or not. Death is not great because it's scary, but because it is profound in its immense capacity to arouse our loving nature, bring attentiveness to the experience of living, and seal the interrelationship between living and dying. When we hear of a death, we are reminded that we are interdependent with one another. There is no silence so sobering as death. We stop and become aware of the loss of life and the loss of ourselves in relationship with a person who no longer exists. Maybe we even realize that the body is just a cover or vehicle needed by our spirit to do the work we are on earth to do.

From the darkness of the dying process, great teachings come. The dying are often able to see life from a different perspective, specifically from a place of possibly never returning to earth. When a Zen priest is dying, they are asked to write a death poem. Their poem is written in the darkest part of life, in which the things and people of the world are being released. Like the fall equinox, when the daylight starts to become shorter and the darkness pervades, the stillness of death brings wisdom we would not gain otherwise. My dharma sister Junsei Osho (Jana Drakka, aka Elizabeth) died in 2018. This was her death poem:

How can you live under these conditions?
—Every breath is a gift.
How can you feel joy with all these conditions?
—Every smile is a gift.

Reading and writing death poems of the Zen tradition provide a glimpse into the experience of letting go, of opening and dropping into infinite blackness. At the moment of death, we are forced to surrender. The dying Zen practitioner then offers us a teaching in the midst of their dying. Many of these poems are about finally attaining a pure heart, or seeing the empty shell of the cicada and knowing it as one's own life, or having been dreaming the entire time while one was alive. After reading death poems, I notice a sense of peace with death and a heart expansion as opposed to the feeling of cowering away from darkness. Although I am not physically dying while reading such poems, I sense the distillation of the nature of darkness in its many forms in life.

In your small and temporary deaths, what blocks your peaceful surrender to the darkness of life? Is it how you see yourself or what you think you know? In dark experiences, can you still find a sense of life as melting snow that is not separate from the darkness?

How we view darkness is tied to how we experience death. We have a tendency to run from what is unavoidable rather than stopping and wondering if we are being haunted by darkness and death or invited into the mystical and magical aspects of existence.

Death and Darkness as Sources of Power

Tomás Prower, a priest of La Santa Muerte (the Spirit of Death), writes, "We are here on earth to be human, not gods. And the human experience involves death, a lesson not to be feared, only understood."[13] Devotees to his spiritual tradition view death as a mystical and magical existence. Although being devoted to the Spirit of Death seemingly venerates the macabre, it is a way of living in the here and now. Devotees of La Santa Muerte learn to enjoy life despite inevitable death, and they view death as a woman who is like a caring mother figure. The spirit of La Santa Muerte is welcoming to all, but her devotees have not always been welcomed in the world. Many keep their practice to themselves, because the Catholic Church has branded their faith as evil and harmful.

To know death is to know the power of our lives. We can use our energy to live rather than suffering our deaths while still alive. The skeleton as an image in La Santa Muerte is not a frightening one, but one that acknowledges exactly who we are in the present moment. Eventually, we discover that we are not even a skeleton. In time, it too will become brittle and leave.

Take fifteen minutes to be with yourself and your vision of death. Afterward, write down what you saw. How are the mysteries of death connected to your life? What can help bring magic to dying for you? Write it down. You may not have the right words. Try to write something down. You can always come back to it later. The purpose here is to initiate you into death, into what is already present with you. To bring you into your life as it is, to destroy whatever is old that prevents transition into the new. Allow the welcoming embrace of Mama Brijit or La Santa Muerte to hold you in the fear that exists because you have not been taught about darkness and the dark medicine that comes from it.

In Bhutanese spirituality, there are messengers called *deloms* who travel into the hell realms to meet Yama, the Lord of the Dead, and bring back messages for the living.[14] Traditionally, these messengers have been women. They have the capacity to leave their bodies and appear dead for some time. Their families keep their bodies warm until they return. These days, some deloms claim to be the reincarnated mediums of famous deloms of the past.

There is the possibility of something new happening in the death of things, if we can be messengers for what the dark is birthing in death. Whether you believe death is final or a transition into the afterlife, it doesn't matter. Death happens anyway. Death is here as the greatest gateway into eternal blackness. In celebrating death, may it mend your severance from darkness and help to reconcile your relationship with everything dark and black.

GUIDED STILLNESS EIGHT

Listening to the Black Rooster
Working with the Black Rooster of Mama Brijit
East Direction
Meditation as Listening

Take your dharma seat in a quiet space in the east direction for the second time. This is the last direction of the mandala. You have gone clockwise and counterclockwise in making a mandala of darkness within your heart.

Take a deep breath and release it slowly. Very slowly. Repeat several times. Then breathe in your own rhythm.

Read the blessing below slowly, breathing between words.

Blessing

May you feel the mother love of Mama Brijit,
a love you may not have felt in this life.
May you be protected and at peace with dying
and feel free to curse it, defy it with rebirth if need be.
Let the spirits of your relatives who have gone before you
meet you at the time you are ready to leave this earth.
May your life be celebrated forever.

Guided Stillness

You will need a journal or pad of paper and a pen for this practice.

We will use the black rooster of Mama Brijit, representing celebration, awareness of darkness and death, and the consciousness of light (awakening) signaled by the crowing of roosters.

Please reflect on an experience when something within you died after you went through dark times. What changed in you that was so great you felt some part of you (or all of you) died and something else of your being came to fruition? Do not judge what left you as good or bad. Let's pause and breathe in and out.

Now imagine you have a black rooster in the backyard where you live. Notice the rooster's comb on its head, its eyes, its red wattles hanging from its throat, its claws, or its black tail feathers. While its crowing has been used to ward off evil and darkness, we will use it now to help us within darkness.

Breathe and observe the rooster's movement.

Now, go back to the time when you were changed so greatly by a dark experience that you felt a significant part of you died. See the rooster as a familiar that is here to help you gather the messages from that death.

Is your rooster crowing? Or did it crow as soon as you began paying attention to it? When you hear the rooster crowing, feel that as a signal that you are still among the living.

Before the dark experience changed you, what words would you have used to describe death? Write them down. Take your time. Breathe. When you are done, try to add more until your pen stops. Once you stop, put your pen down and listen to your rooster crowing. It's saying, "We are still here." Listen to the crowing wind up and fade into nothingness. Let the words you have written down fade into nothing with the crowing. The paper will hold them for you.

Stillness and breathing. Stillness and breathing.

Now think of the occasion after the experience that felt like a death. What words would you use *now* to describe death? Write them in your journal or on a pad of paper. Breathe. Take your time. Keep writing until your pen stops. Put your pen down and listen to your rooster crowing. It's saying, "We are still here." As before, listen to the crowing rise and fall into nothingness. Let the words you have written down fade into nothing, too.

Stillness and breathing. Stillness and breathing.

Now allow the rooster to be your spiritual mirror, reflecting your inner world. What do you see of yourself after death? Write it down. Use as few words as possible to describe what you see through the eyes of the rooster. Once you stop, put your pen down and listen to your rooster crowing. Listen to the crowing wind up and fade into nothingness. Let the words you have written down fade into nothing with the crowing.

Can you celebrate your successful death? Can we invite the unknown of death and trust its pervasive capacity to change and guide us? Hear the rooster crowing. Keep hearing it until it fades into nothing, the nothing that death is.

Now let go of all the words you have written down. You can throw them away or paste a photo or illustration of a rooster over the words in your journal.

Next, take some time to read out loud, slowly, the following meditation.

Meditation

I know dying as life,
and I realize the seeds planted in the womb of darkness
will bring birth and in death sustain the lineage
of ancestors forever.
I open to darkness,
I open to the mystical and magical birth of death,
I open to the renewal and awakening beyond this life.

Please pause here and breathe slowly. Thank you for having gone through the eight gateways. I send a warm embrace. Of course, you can return to the gateways over and over, each time building on whatever foundation you have made to navigate dark times. It takes courage to accept darkness in all of its forms, but we can relish its unlimited possibilities. Move forward in peace with the mandala of darkness within you. Congratulations.

PART 3

OPENING TO THE ABSENCE OF LIGHT

In the beginning, the dark water of the womb was home.
Without ears, eyes, a nose, a tongue, without light, there
    was still sight, smell, sound, taste, and touch.
We descended in birth from the great mystery of the dark,
    making us rich and full with the forever unknown.

In the dark waters of our beginnings, we did not
    know light, so there was no fear of darkness.
Life was dark, and we rested in it.
In this place of origin, we still live, massive
    blackness surrounding us, not good or bad,
    itself unattached to light, yet related.

Upon our birth, light was as unknown as the
    darkness from which we came.
Radiance, bright to our new eyes and body, was
    undefinable, and we were left to explore this light in
    the same way we explored our home of darkness.
We were without words, uncertain of the
    light or the dark we speak of.

The light that can and cannot be seen with
    these eyes is as unknown as the dark.
Our world lit up upon our birth, and still we do not
    remember the first light beyond the sun and the moon.

We can know only a kind of light with these
    eyes that were formed in darkness, a kind of
    light we could never create or conjure.

Eyes closed, we remember the stillness of our
    beginnings, filled with sound without speech,
    movement without a destination.
The smell and feel of flesh, bone, and muscle gave
    texture to blackness, by which we could touch life.
We still can see into darkness, not with the eyes
    that are closed or open, but with the sight
    given in the darkness of our birth.*

---

*   I wrote this poetic prayer at the onset of the coronavirus pandemic.

A CALL FOR RECONCILIATION WITH DARKNESS AND BLACKNESS

Please continue to reconcile your relationship with darkness. Are you ready to be with darkness as a companion in the way you have allowed light to be?

As I wrote in the opening of this book, "This journey is not a call to those who want to stay in what they think is light in order to avoid being negative or being consumed by the dark where monsters and monstrous things live. It is not for those who think they can give light through their words, songs, or cheery dispositions. It is not for those who want to remain wedded to the fear and/or not willing to reconsider that which they were taught in relationship to darkness. This call is not for those who are interested in sustaining some imagined protection from darkness. It is for the brave ones, the ones who remember living in dark times as a place of power and clear seeing."

This is a call to those who sense a disconnection with darkness and want to reconcile a spiritual relationship with it. I have no interest here in convincing anyone of anything, other than to reveal to you that if you have *any* disdain for darkness it transfers over to an avoidance of dark experiences, dark things, and dark people. It is an avoidance of life itself.

These Eight Gateways of exploring darkness are open to assist you. I'm sure there are more. There is no peace in running from darkness. This call is offered in love and protection. If your heart is right, there is nothing to fear. If you truly walk with God or any other creator or source of life, then there is nothing to be afraid of here. Listen, if only for a moment, to the necessary call for these difficult times and for the difficult times ahead. It is a necessary call from the dark mothers, ancestors, and Mother Earth herself for us to do more than pay attention, do more than commit to justice, and do more than meditate to relieve ourselves. It is a call to cease pointing out things and people as the problem and to see our dark experiences as coming from the primordial darkness from which everything was given birth—the wrong, the right, the good, and the bad.

There is a common ground in the darkness. We do not know anything until it has come from the darkness. We do not know light until it has been shaped by the darkness. We cannot expect to be saved—either from ourselves or from one another—or to save the earth without understanding and opening to the existence of darkness and blackness called life. There is good reason for this call. We are seeking more than salvation as more people are awakening.

It doesn't matter if you are Christian, Buddhist, Muslim, Hindu, Wiccan, Vodou practitioner, atheist, or pagan; follow a Native American tradition; or are a child of the African orishas. You may consider yourself nonspiritual or nonreligious. It only matters that you are here on this planet. It matters that we are aligned with the earth in holding everyone and everything in this union with darkness. Some may harm others willfully or unconsciously as a result of past wounding, some may ignore the depletion of the earth's resources, and some find power in a false sense of superiority. Still, we can all recognize our coexistence within darkness. This is the beginning of opening to darkness, opening to that which we all live within. To look at blackness in its face and know that all living beings experience darkness of some kind—in some place, every day—is to see all of humanity, all living beings. Mother Earth may pardon us if we access the darkness that is always present, and if we co-create with her in darkness, and if we honor the ground that everyone walks together, whether they enjoy the walk or not. What is there to enjoy other than the fact that we have arrived here and were given everything from the earth by which to live? Earth gives us her very breath.

There is no road map in opening to darkness. There is only your prayer, your call, your cry, your wisdom. These will lead you in the wilderness back to your wild self—the being who once knew how to crawl in the dark, not looking for light, but being with darkness knowing light is there. This wild self is a person who does not need to be preached to or taught as long as the darkness is remembered.

No one can answer or call to you other than yourself. We cannot ask the person next to us to befriend darkness for us, to bring its light to us. Even though others can join us and our interrelationship is inherent, the call is a solo journey, an inward turning that cannot be done by anyone else. No one else can do your healing for you. We are accountable to our own bodies, minds, and spirits. If we don't accept such responsibility, a reconciliation to darkness and blackness for humanity is not possible. We will wander in ignorance, not knowing we are home in the darkness. We are in training at home in the darkness. Training for what? For life.

Anyone who can open to darkness is a true seeker. Seekers are alike in that they reach into the mystery of life each time they make an inquiry or make a step away from certainty (and therefore toward discovery). The first act of life is dwelling in the darkness of our mother's womb. The second act is coming from the darkness into more darkness, as we do not know the world upon entrance. And thus, we seek. We cry out for guidance and assistance. We seek refuge. We are constantly morphing into newness, and yet the ancient, primordial darkness remains as a wonderland for us to wander in, discovering the magic of this life. Once the seeker turns to the darkness and is embraced by darkness rather than chased, the warmth causes the seeker to weep. In seeking, you will find; in being, you will be found. There is excitement in seeking oneself in darkness, and tears of joy come when you are found in darkness and there is no more seeking.

We are on an eternal pilgrimage of the intangible. We are constantly in unfamiliar territory without answers. This can be paralyzing, or it can be an invitation to take a deep dive into yourself. Darkness comes into our lives, personally and collectively, to take us off the course of longing and desire. In essence, it is sobering. The madness created by darkness has a purpose. Looking into what cannot be grasped is to take a risk. What will you find? Who will you find?

Now, consider darkness, not as darkness, not as blackness, not as light, not as the bare season of winter, but as something without a name, without a deity. Consider darkness before breath, as simply the great suspension. Consider that the ever-increasing darkness on the planet is calling us away from our clinging, suspending us in the ancient cosmos, in the unknown that was before us. Consider that we are being called to enter the middle of nowhere, to follow nothing into nothingness, into deathlessness. To open into openness, to open into an eternal eclipse that appears dark and empty but is filled with the unseen and the unknowable.

Sit quietly in the dark. Sit quietly in dark experiences. Sit quietly with dark matters and see what is there without making an effort to see anything. Be the mystic. Be the monk. Connect to the wisdom of darkness through contemplating it and then surrendering to it without effort. Darkness has come on its own seeking you. Perhaps you have called in darkness without knowing it.

The call is to reconcile with darkness, to ease your fear. Darkness resides in people, places, and inner journeys. Dark times are continuous and have been since the beginning of time. As long as there is birth and death, there are dark times. What are you to do with this dark friend you may have made into a stranger? Invite the stranger in for a tea and a talk. Invite the darkness that loves you, that comes to you with sword and flowers, that shows you who you are. The darkness will not leave you, because it loves you. It is you.

Sacred darkness. Abundant darkness. Illuminating darkness. Chaotic darkness. Primordial darkness. Good versus bad darkness. We grab onto these names attached to darkness. I myself have used, even here, many of these names for darkness, if only to be a bridge of understanding and to invite you into something that has caused many of us to fall on our knees or cry out in protest. You may name the darkness of your experience and then grab onto that so that you can understand your experience. You may try to experience the nothingness, as well. But darkness has no description or name, really, and it can't be owned or grabbed onto. It can appear light, but it is not light. It is dark, but not dark.

What is darkness? Can you allow it to be ever evolving as it teaches you? Can it go unnamed in your fear of it? Can you allow it to make you tremble long enough to show you its kind but sometimes harsh nature? We know how it feels, which helps make healers, messengers, and mystics of us, if only for ourselves.

Scream into darkness, wail if you must. But we can't continue running from what hurts, from what scares us. Next time you look up into the sky and see the stars, know that some of the brightest ones have been dead for some time. It is a mystery. We are mysteries, especially in dark times.

We have come into life without understanding what life is. Where did we come from? Where are we going? Without the answers we are frightened. With the answers we are frightened. The difficulties are part of life. No difficulties mean we are not alive. No disruptions mean we will not change. What joy we could have in working together with what challenges us as people. When it truly no longer matters what our appearance is, based on the color of our skin, based on gender, or based on anything else concocted or fixated upon by human beings, a distorted darkness will be replaced in this world with the pure darkness from which we were born. We will struggle, but the struggle will be of a different kind, not of our own making. Darkness will come from the earth and not be the darkness of our creation, something small and tragic. This darkness from the earth will lead to expansion of consciousness, which is expansion of light.

This call to darkness is not meant to harm or frighten you any more than you have already been frightened in your life. This call is meant to reduce the feeling of being haunted by dark experiences, by what you haven't been able to welcome into your life. Everything that life brings can be used to see further into this life. If you say you love darkness and blackness, then look to see if you love your struggle as a human being in the same way.

Our pain, suffering, and discombobulation are meant to help us commit to our lives and be willing to help others. In darkness, we become devoted to clarity, courage, peace, and harmony. We discover the basic goodness of all humanity when we experience darkness together, which is to experience life together. The darkness can be the mess between us or the veil that protects our radiance. That veil is lifted at the right time for the benefit of all. Our personal use of light disappears.

When darkness comes in the form of difficulties, unwelcomed events, and people, breathe into that darkness that is vast as the night. It looks empty, but the dark sky is full of life. The darkness has come to assist you in connecting with everyone and everything that has come from such darkness and will return. These difficulties, unwelcomed events, and people come to everyone. Darkness comes to everyone as a great connector, because we all have come from it. The greatest courage is to open to darkness, to see all that life brings, whether it is acceptable or not. When darkness is welcomed, then nothing and no one is rejected.

Facing darkness is not for the faint of heart. I believe this work will bring us together as human beings as we come to understand darkness and blackness in our lives and in the world. What I have seen in my years is that some become friends in dark times—at least those who are willing to see themselves as coexisting on this planet. We have lost a lot together. Only together will we thrive on this planet.

I continue to answer this call over and over, for the sake of all humanity and for all living beings. Will you?

NOTES

1. Andrew Harvey, *Experience Renewal Through the Global Dark Night: Finding Your Purpose and Strength by Embracing the Mystical Meaning Behind the Crisis*, podcast, produced by the Shift Network, September 26, 2020.

2. Michael Meade, "The Darkness Around Us," *Living Myth*, podcast, episode 209, January 8, 2021, mosaicvoices.org /episode-209-the-darkness-around-us.

3. Lorna J. Marshall, *Nyae Nyae !Kung: Beliefs and Rites* (Cambridge, MA: Peabody Museum Press, 1999).

4. Personal telephone conversation with Miranda Shaw, July 2020.

5. Zenju Earthlyn Manuel, *The Deepest Peace: Contemplations from a Season of Stillness* (San Francisco: Parallax Press, 2020).

6. Jake Skeets, "The Other House: Musings on the Diné Perspective of Time," *Emergence Magazine*, April 29, 2020, emergencemagazine.org/essay/the-other-house/.

7. Marina Magloire, "The Spirit Writing of Lucille Clifton," *Paris Review*, October 19, 2020, theparisreview.org/blog/2020/10/19 /the-spirit-writing-of-lucille-clifton/.

8. Eckhart Tolle, *Teachings on "Being the Light,"* YouTube, September 25, 2020, 20:02, youtube.com/watch?v=Ypv5nEBBRYg.

9. Adyashanti, *The End of Your World: Uncensored Straight Talk on the Nature of Enlightenment* (Boulder, CO: Sounds True, 2010).

10. Emilie Townes, *Womanist Ethics and the Cultural Production of Evil* (London: Palgrave Macmillan, 2007).

11. "Let Us Make Sanctuary," interview with Bayo Akomolafe, *Insights at the Edge*, podcast, produced by Sounds True, September 30, 2020.

12. Tsultrim Allione, *Feeding Your Demons: Ancient Wisdom for Resolving Inner Conflict* (New York: Little, Brown Spark, 2008).

13. Tomás Prower, *La Santa Muerte: Unearthing the Magic and Mysticism of Death* (Woodbury, MN: Llewellyn Publications, 2015).

14. Stephanie Guyer-Stevens and Françoise Pommaret, *Divine Messengers: The Untold Story of Bhutan's Female Shamans* (Boulder, CO: Shambhala Publications, 2021).

ABOUT THE AUTHOR

ZENJU EARTHLYN MANUEL, PhD, is an author, poet, and ordained Zen Buddhist priest. Her books include *The Shamanic Bones of Zen*, *The Deepest Peace, Sanctuary, The Way of Tenderness*, and *Tell Me Something about Buddhism*. She writes and teaches from her experience of Zen rituals, African and Native American indigenous ceremonies, and her own awakening at the intersection of spirituality, transformation, and divine justice. For more information, visit zenju.org.

ABOUT SOUNDS TRUE

Sounds True is a multimedia publisher whose mission is to inspire and support personal transformation and spiritual awakening. Founded in 1985 and located in Boulder, Colorado, we work with many of the leading spiritual teachers, thinkers, healers, and visionary artists of our time. We strive with every title to preserve the essential "living wisdom" of the author or artist. It is our goal to create products that not only provide information to a reader or listener but also embody the quality of a wisdom transmission.

For those seeking genuine transformation, Sounds True is your trusted partner. At SoundsTrue.com you will find a wealth of free resources to support your journey, including exclusive weekly audio interviews, free downloads, interactive learning tools, and other special savings on all our titles.

To learn more, please visit SoundsTrue.com/freegifts or call us toll-free at 800.333.9185.